UNIFORM WITH THIS VOLUME.

A PRESENT HEAVEN.

BY THE SAME AUTHOR.

TICKNOR AND FIELDS, Publishers.

THE

PATIENCE OF HOPE

BY

THE AUTHOR OF "A PRESENT HEAVEN"

WITH AN INTRODUCTION

BY

JOHN G. WHITTIER

ET TENEO ET TENEOR

BOSTON
TICKNOR AND FIELDS
1863

FIFTH EDITION.

UNIVERSITY PRESS:
WELCH, BIGELOW, AND COMPANY
CAMBRIDGE.

INTRODUCTION.

THERE are men who, irrespective of the names by which they are called in the Babel confusion of sects, are endeared to the common heart of Christendom. Our doors open of their own accord to receive them. For in them we feel that in some faint degree, and with many limitations, the Divine is again manifested : something of the Infinite Love shines out of them ; their very garments have healing and fragrance borrowed from the bloom of Paradise. So of books. There are volumes which perhaps contain many things, in the matter of doctrine and illustration, to which our reason does not assent, but which nevertheless seem permeated with a certain sweetness and savor of life. They have the Divine seal and imprimatur ; they are fragrant with heart's-ease and asphodel ; tonic with the leaves which are for the healing of the na-

tions. The meditations of the devout monk of
Kempen are the common heritage of Catholic
and Protestant; our hearts burn within us as we
walk with Augustine under Numidian fig-trees
in the gardens of Verecundus; Fenelon from
his bishop's palace, and John Woolman from
his tailor's shop, speak to us in the same language. The unknown author of that book
which Luther loved next to his Bible, the
"Theologia Germanica" is just as truly at
home in this present age, and in the ultra Protestantism of New England, as in the heart of
Catholic Europe, and in the fourteenth century.
For such books know no limitations of time
or place; they have the perpetual freshness and
fitness of truth; they speak out of profound
experience: heart answers to heart as we read
them; the spirit that is in man, and the inspira-
tion that giveth understanding, bear witness to
them. The bent and stress of their testimony
are the same, whether written in this or a past
century, by Catholic or Quaker: self-renuncia-
tion, — reconcilement to the Divine will through
simple faith in the Divine goodness, and the
love of it which must needs follow its recognition, — the life of Christ made our own by self-
denial and sacrifice, and the fellowship of his
suffering for the good of others, — the indwell-

ing Spirit, leading into all truth, — the Divine Word nigh us, even in our hearts. They have little to do with creeds, or schemes of doctrine, or the partial and inadequate plans of salvation invented by human speculation and ascribed to Him who — it is sufficient to know — is able to save unto the uttermost all who trust in him. They insist upon simple faith and holiness of life, rather than rituals or modes of worship; they leave the merely formal, ceremonial, and temporal part of religion to take care of itself, and earnestly seek for the substantial, the necessary, and the permanent.

With these legacies of devout souls, it seems to me, the little volume herewith presented is not wholly unworthy of a place. It assumes the life and power of the Gospel as a matter of actual experience; it bears unmistakable evidence of a realization, on the part of its author, of the truth, that Christianity is not simply historical and traditional, but present and permanent, with its roots in the infinite past and its branches in the infinite future, the eternal spring and growth of Divine love; not the dying echo of words uttered centuries ago, never to be repeated, but God's good tidings spoken afresh in every soul, — the perennial fountain and unstinted outflow of wisdom and goodness, forever old and forever new. It is a lofty plea for patience, trust, hope, and holy confidence, under the shadow, as well as in the light, of Christian experience, whether the cloud seems to rest on the tabernacle, or moves guidingly forward. It is perhaps too exclusively addressed to those who minister in the inner sanctuary, to be entirely intelligible to the vaster number who wait in the outer courts ; it overlooks, perhaps, too much the solidarity and oneness of humanity ; * but all who read it will feel its earnestness, and confess to the singular beauty of its style, the strong, steady march of its argument, and the wide and varied learning which illustrates it. To use the language of one of its reviewers in the Scottish press : —

"Beauty there is in the book ; exquisite glimpses into the loveliness of nature here and there shine out from its lines, — a charm wanting which meditative writing always seems to have a defect ; beautiful gleams, too, there are of the choicest things of art, and frequent allusions by the way to legend or picture of the religious past ; so that, while you read, you

* "The good are not so good as I once thought, nor the bad so evil, and in all there is more for grace to make advantage of, and more to testify for God and holiness, than I once believed." — *Baxter.*

wander by a clear brook of thought, coming
far from the beautiful hills, and winding away
from beneath the sunshine of gladness and
beauty into the dense, mysterious forest of human existence, that loves to sing, amid the
shadow of human darkness and anguish, its
music of heaven-born consolation ; bringing,
too, its pure waters of cleansing and healing,
yet evermore making its praise of holy affection and gladness ; while it is still haunted by
the spirits of prophet, saint, and poet, repeat-
ing snatches of their strains, and is led on, as
by a spirit from above, to join the great river
of God's truth. . . . . .

"This is a book for Christian men, for the
quiet hour of holy solitude, when the heart
longs and waits for access to the presence of
the Master. The weary heart that thirsts
amidst its conflicts and its toils for refreshing
water, will drink eagerly of these sweet and
refreshing words. To thoughtful men and
women, especially such as have learnt any of
the patience of hope in the experiences of sorrow and trial, we commend this little volume
most heartily and earnestly."

"The Patience of Hope" fell into my hands
soon after its publication in Edinburgh, some

1 *

two years ago. I was at once impressed by
its extraordinary richness of language and imagery, — its deep and solemn tone of meditation in rare combination with an eminent-
ly practical tendency, — philosophy warm and
glowing with love. It will, perhaps, be less the
fault of the writer than of her readers, if they
are not always able to eliminate from her
highly poetical and imaginative language the
subtle metaphysical verity or phase of religious
experience which she seeks to express, or that
they are compelled to pass over, without ap-
propriation, many things which are nevertheless
profoundly suggestive as vague possibilities of
the highest life. All may not be able to find
in some of her Scriptural citations the exact
weight and significance so apparent to her own
mind. She startles us, at times, by her novel
applications of familiar texts, by meanings reflected upon them from her own spiritual intuitions, making the barren Baca of the letter
a well. If the rendering be questionable, the
beauty and quaint felicity of illustration and
comparison are unmistakable ; and we call to
mind Augustine's saying, that two or more
widely varying interpretations of Scripture may
be alike true in themselves considered. " When
one saith, ' Moses meant as I do,' and an-

other saith, ' Nay, but as I do,' I ask, more reverently, ' Why not rather as both, if both be true ? ' "

Some minds, for instance, will hesitate to assent to the use of certain Scriptural passages, as evidence that He who is the Light of men, the Way and the Truth, in the mystery of his economy, designedly " delays, withdraws, and even hides himself from those who love and follow him." They will prefer to impute spiritual dearth and darkness to human weakness, to the selfishness which seeks a sign for itself, to evil imaginations indulged, to the taint and burden of some secret sin, or to some disease and exaggeration of the conscience, growing out of bodily infirmity, rather than to any purpose on the part of our Heavenly Father to perplex and mislead his children. The sun does not shine the less because one side of our planet is in darkness. To borrow the words of Augustine : " Thou, Lord, forsakest nothing thou hast made. Thou alone art near to those even who remove far from thee. Let them turn and seek thee, for not as they have forsaken their Creator hast thou forsaken thy creation." It is only by holding fast the thought of Infinite Goodness, and interpreting doubtful Scripture and inward spiritual experience by the light of that central idea, that we can altogether escape the dreadful conclusion of Pascal, that revelation has been given us in dubious cipher, contradictory and mystical, in order that some, through miraculous aid, may understand it to their salvation, and others be mystified by it to their eternal loss.

I might mention other points of probable divergence between reader and writer, and indicate more particularly my own doubtful pause and hesitancy over some of these pages. But it is impossible for me to make one to whom I am so deeply indebted an offender for a word or a Scriptural rendering. On the grave and awful themes which she discusses, I have little to say in the way of controversy. I would listen, rather than criticise. The utterances of pious souls, in all ages, are to me often like fountains in a thirsty land, strengthening and refreshing, yet not without an after-taste of human frailty and inadequateness, a slight bitterness of disappointment and unsatisfied quest. Who has not felt at times that the letter killeth, that prophecies fail, and tongues cease to edify, and been ready to say, with the author of the " Imitation of Christ ": " Speak, Lord, for thy servant heareth. Let not Moses nor the prophets speak to me, but speak thou rather, who art the Inspirer and Enlightener of all. I am weary with reading and hearing many things; let all teachers hold their peace; let all creatures keep silence: speak thou alone to me."

The writer of "The Patience of Hope" had, previous to its publication, announced herself to a fit, if small, audience of earnest and thoughtful Christians, in a little volume entitled, "A Present Heaven." She has recently published a collection of poems, of which so competent a judge as Dr. Brown, the author of "Horæ Subsecivæ" and "Rab and his Friends," thus speaks, in the North British Review: —

"Such of our readers — a fast increasing number — as have read and enjoyed 'The Patience of Hope,' listening to the gifted nature which, through such deep and subtile thought, and through affection and godliness still deeper and more quick, has charmed and soothed them, will not be surprised to learn that she is not only poetical, but, what is more, a poet, and one as true as George Herbert and Henry Vaughan, or our own Cowper; for, with all our admiration of the searching, fearless speculation, the wonderful power of speaking clearly upon dark and all but unspeakable subjects, the rich outcome of 'thoughts that wander through eternity,' which increases every time we take up that wonderful little book, we confess we were surprised at the kind and the amount of true poetic *vis* in these poems, from the same fine and strong hand. There is a personality and immediateness, a sort of sacredness and privacy, as if they were overheard rather than read, which gives to these remarkable productions a charm and a flavor all their own. With no effort, no consciousness of any end but that of uttering the inmost thoughts and desires of the heart, they flow out as clear, as living, as gladdening as the wayside well, coming from out the darkness of the central depths, filtered into purity by time and travel. The waters are copious, sometimes to overflowing; but they are always limpid and unforced, singing their own quiet tune, not saddening, though sometimes sad, and their darkness not that of obscurity, but of depth, like that of the deep sea.

"This is not a book to criticise or speak about, and we give no extracts from the longer, and in this case, we think, the better poems. In reading this *Cardiphonia* set to music, we have been often reminded, not only of Herbert and Vaughan, but of Keble, — a likeness of the spirit, not of the letter; for if there is any one poet who has given a bent to her mind, it is

Wordsworth, — the greatest of all our century's poets, both in himself and in his power of making poets."

In the belief that whoever peruses the following pages will be sufficiently interested in their author to be induced to turn back and read over again, with renewed pleasure, extracts from her metrical writings, I copy from the volume so warmly commended a few brief pieces and extracts from the longer poems.

Here are three sonnets, each a sermon in itself : —

ASCENDING.

THEY who from mountain-peaks have gazed upon
   The wide, illimitable heavens, have said,
   That, still receding as they climbed, outspread,
The blue vault deepens over them, and, one
By one drawn further back, each starry sun
   Shoots down a feebler splendor overhead.
   So, Saviour, as our mounting spirits, led
Along Faith's living way to Thee, have won
A nearer access, up the difficult track
   Still pressing, on that rarer atmosphere,
When low beneath us flits the cloudy rack,
   We see Thee drawn within a widening sphere
Of glory, from us further, further back, —
   Yet is it then because we are more *near*.

LIFE TAPESTRY.

Too long have I, methought, with tearful eye
   Pored o'er this tangled work of mine, and mused
   Above each stitch awry and thread confused;
Now will I think on what in years gone by
I heard of them that weave rare tapestry
At royal looms, and how they constant use
To work on the rough side, and still peruse
The pictured pattern set above them high;
So will I set MY COPY high above,
   And gaze and gaze till on my spirit grows
Its gracious impress; till some line of love,
   Transferred upon my canvas, faintly glows;
Nor look too much on warp or woof, provide
He whom I work for sees their fairer side!

HOPE.

When I do think on thee, sweet Hope, and how
   Thou followest on our steps, a coaxing child
   Oft chidden hence, yet quickly reconciled,
Still turning on us a glad, beaming brow,
And red, ripe lips for kisses: even now
   Thou mindest me of him, the Ruler mild,
   Who led God's chosen people through the wild.
And bore with wayward murmurers, meek as thou
That bringest waters from the Rock, with bread
   Of angels strewing Earth for us! like him
   Thy force abates not, nor thine eye grows dim;
But still with milk and honey-droppings fed,
   Thou leadest to the Promised Country fair,
   Though thou, like Moses, may'st not enter *there!*

There is something very weird and striking
in the following lines : —

GONE.

ALONE, at midnight as he knelt, his spirit was aware
Of Somewhat falling in between the silence and the
    prayer ;

A bell's dull clangor that hath sped so far, it faints
    and dies
So soon as it hath reached the ear whereto its errand
    lies ;

And as he rose up from his knees, his spirit was
    aware
Of Somewhat, forceful and unseen, that sought to
    hold him there ;

As of a Form that stood behind, and on his shoulders
    prest
Both hands to stay his rising up, and Somewhat in
    his breast,

In accents clearer far than words, spake, " Pray yet
    longer, pray,
For one that ever prayed for thee this night hath
    passed away ;

" A soul, that climbing hour by hour the silver-
    shining stair
That leads to God's great treasure-house, grew covet-
    ous ; and there

B

" Was stored no blessing and no boon, for thee she
 did not claim,
(So lowly, yet importunate!) and ever with *thy*
 name

" She link'd — that none in earth or heaven might
 hinder it or stay —
One Other Name, so strong, that thine hath never
 missed its way.

" This very night within my arms this gracious soul
 I bore
Within the Gate, where many a prayer of hers had
 gone before ;

" And where she resteth, evermore one constant
 song they raise
Of 'Holy, holy,' so that *now* I know not if she
 prays ;

" But for the voice of praise in Heaven, a voice of
 Prayer hath gone
From Earth ; thy name upriseth now no more ;
 pray on, pray on ! "

The following may serve as a specimen of
the writer's lighter, half-playful strain of mor-
alizing : —

SEEKING.

" And where, and among what pleasant places,
 Have ye been, that ye come again

With your laps so full of flowers, and your faces
   Like buds blown fresh after rain ? "
" We have been," said the children speaking
   In their gladness, as the birds chime,
All together, — " we have been seeking
   For the Fairies of olden time ;
For we thought, they are only hidden, —
   They would never surely go
From this green earth all unbidden,
   And the children that love them so ;
Though they come not around us leaping,
   As they did when they and the world
Were young, we shall find them sleeping
   Within some broad leaf curled ;
For the lily its white doors closes
   But only over the bee,
And we looked through the summer roses,
   Leaf by leaf, so carefully ;
But we thought, rolled up we shall find them
   Among mosses old and dry ;
From gossamer threads that bind them,
   They will start like the butterfly,
All winged : so we went forth seeking,
   Yet still they have kept unseen ;
Though we think our feet have been keeping
   The track where they have been,
For we saw where their dance went flying
   O'er the pastures, — snowy white
Their seats and their tables lying,
   O'erthrown in their sudden flight.

And they, too, have had their losses,
  For we found the goblets white
And red in the old spiked mosses,
  That they drank from over-night;
And in the pale horn of the woodbine
  Was some wine left, clear and bright;
But we found," said the children, speaking
  More quickly, " so many things, —
That we soon forgot we were seeking, —
  Forgot all the Fairy rings,
Forgot all the stories olden
  That we hear round the fire at night,
Of their gifts and their favors golden, —
  The sunshine was so bright;
And the flowers — we found so many
  That it almost made us grieve
To think there were some, sweet as any,
  That we were forced to leave;
As we left, by the brook-side lying,
  The balls of drifted foam,
And brought (after all our trying)
  These Guelder-roses home."

" Then, oh!" I heard one speaking
  Beside me soft and low,
" I have been, like the blessed children, seeking,
  Still seeking, to and fro;
Yet not, like them, for the Fairies, —
  They might pass unmourned away
For me, that had looked on angels —
  On angels that would not stay;

No ! not though in haste before them
  I spread all my heart's best cheer,
And made love my banner o'er them,
  If it might but keep them *here* ;
They stayed but awhile to rest them ;
  Long, long before its close,
From my feast, though I mourned and prest them,
  The radiant guests arose ;
And their flitting wings struck sadness
  And silence ; never more
Hath my soul won back the gladness,
  That was its own before.
No ; I mourned not for the Fairies
  When I had seen hopes decay,
That were sweet unto my spirit
  So long ; I said, ' If they,
That through shade and sunny weather
  Have twined about my heart,
Should fade, we must go together,
  For we can never part ! '
But my care was not availing,
  I found their sweetness gone ;
I saw their bright tints paling ; —
  They died ; yet I lived on.

" Yet seeking, ever seeking
  Like the children, I have won
A guerdon all undreamt of
  When first my quest begun,
And my thoughts come back like wanderers,
  Out-wearied, to my breast ;

What they sought for long they found not,
  Yet was the Unsought best.
For I sought not out for crosses,
  I did not seek for pain ;
Yet I find the heart's sore losses
  Were the spirit's surest gain."

In "A Meditation," the writer ventures, not
without awe and reverence, upon that dim, un-
sounded ocean of mystery, the life beyond.

         " But is there prayer
Within your quiet Homes, and is there care
For those ye leave behind ?   I would address
My spirit to this theme in humbleness :
  No tongue nor pen hath uttered or made known
This mystery, and thus I do but guess
  At clearer types through lowlier patterns shown ;
Yet when did Love on earth forsake its own ?
  Ye may not quit your sweetness, in the Vine
  More firmly rooted than of old, your wine
Hath freer flow ! ye have not changed, but grown
To fuller stature ; though the shock was keen
That severed you from us, how oft below
Hath sorest parting smitten but to show
True hearts their hidden wealth that quickly grow
The closer for that anguish, — friend to friend
Revealed more clear, — and what is Death to rend
The ties of life and love, when He must fade
In light of very Life, when He must bend
To love, that, loving, loveth to the end ?

I do not deem ye look
Upon us now, for be it that your eyes
Are sealed or clear, a burden on them lies
   Too deep and blissful for their gaze to brook
Our troubled strife ; enough that once ye dwelt
Where now we dwell, enough that once ye felt
As now we feel, to bid you recognize
Our claim of kindred cherished though unseen ;
   And Love that is to you for eye and ear
   Hath ways unknown to us to bring you near, —
To keep you near for all that comes between ;
As pious souls that move in sleep to prayer,
As distant friends, that see not, and yet share
(I speak of what I know) each other's care,
So may your spirits blend with ours ! above
Ye know not haply of our state, yet Love
Acquaints you with our need, and through a way
More sure than that of knowledge — so ye pray !

   And even thus we meet,
And even thus we commune ! spirits freed
And spirits fettered mingle, nor have need
To seek a common atmosphere, the air
   Is meet for either in this olden, sweet,
Primeval breathing of Man's spirit, — Prayer !

   I give, in conclusion, a portion of one of her
most characteristic poems, " The Reconciler."

   Our dreams are reconciled,
Since Thou didst come to turn them all to Truth ;

The World, the Heart, are dreamers in their youth
  Of visions beautiful, and strange and wild ;
And Thou, our Life's Interpreter, dost still
At once make clear these visions and fulfil ;
    Each dim sweet Orphic rhyme,
    Each mythic tale sublime
Of strength to save, of sweetness to subdue,
    Each morning dream the few,
Wisdom's first lovers told, if read in Thee comes true.

    .   .   .   .

    Thou, O Friend
From heaven, that madest this our heart Thine own,
Dost pierce the broken language of its moan —
Thou dost not scorn our needs, but satisfy !
    Each yearning deep and wide,
    Each claim, is justified ;
Our young illusions fail not, though they die
  Within the brightness of Thy Rising, kissed
To happy death, like early clouds that lie
  About the gates of Dawn, — a golden mist
Paling to blissful white, through rose and amethyst.

    The World that puts Thee by,
That opens not to greet Thee with Thy train,
  That sendeth after Thee the sullen cry,
" We will not have thee over us to reign " ;
Itself doth testify through searchings vain
Of Thee and of its need, and for the good
It will not, of some base similitude
Takes up a taunting witness, till its mood,

Grown fierce o'er failing hopes, doth rend and tear
Its own illusions grown too thin and bare
To wrap it longer ; for within the gate
Where all must pass, a veiled and hooded Fate
A dark Chimera, coiled and tangled lies,
And he who answers not its questions dies, —
Still changing form and speech, but with the same
Vexed riddles, Gordian-twisted, bringing shame
Upon the nations that with eager cry
Hail each new solver of the mystery ;
 Yet he, of these the best,
 Bold guesser, hath but prest
Most nigh to Thee, our noisy plaudits wrong ;
 True Champion, that hast wrought
 Our help of old, and brought
Meat from this eater, sweetness from this strong.

  O Bearer of the key
That shuts and opens with a sound so sweet
Its turning in the wards is melody,
All things we move among are incomplete
And vain until we fashion them in Thee !
We labor in the fire,
 Thick smoke is round about us, through the din
Of words that darken counsel clamors dire
 Ring from thought's beaten anvil, where within
Two Giants toil, that even from their birth
With travail-pangs have torn their mother Earth,
And wearied out her children with their keen
Upbraidings of the other, till between

   2

Thou camest, saying, " Wherefore do ye wrong
Each other ?—ye are Brethren."   Then these twain
Will own their kindred, and in Thee retain
Their claims in peace, because Thy land is wide
As it is goodly ! here they pasture free,
This lion and this leopard, side by side,
A little child doth lead them with a song ;
Now, Ephraim's envy ceaseth, and no more
Doth Judah anger Ephraim chiding sore,
For one did ask a Brother, one a King,
So dost Thou gather them in one, and bring —
Thou, King forevermore, forever Priest,
Thou, Brother of our own from bonds released —
    A Law of Liberty,
    A Service making free,
A Commonweal where each has all in Thee.

    And not alone these wide,
Deep-planted yearnings, seeking with a cry
Their meat from God, in Thee are satisfied ;
But all our instincts waking suddenly
Within the soul, like infants from their sleep
That stretch their arms into the dark and weep,
Thy voice can still.   The stricken heart bereft
Of all its brood of singing hopes, and left
'Mid leafless boughs, a cold, forsaken nest
With snow-flakes in it, folded in thy breast
Doth lose its deadly chill ; and grief that creeps
Unto thy side for shelter, finding there

The wound's deep cleft, forgets its moan, and weeps
Calm, quiet tears, and on thy forehead Care
Hath looked until its thorns, no longer bare,
Put forth pale roses.   Pain on thee doth press
Its quivering cheek, and all the weariness,
The want that keep their silence, till from Thee
They hear the gracious summons, none beside
Hath spoken to the world-worn, " Come to me,"
Tell forth their heavy secrets.

   Thou dost hide
These in thy bosom, and not these alone,
But all our heart's fond treasure that had grown
A burden else : O Saviour, tears were weighed
To Thee in plenteous measure ! none hath shown
That Thou didst smile ! yet hast Thou surely made
All joy of ours Thine own ;

    Thou madest us for Thine ;
We seek amiss, we wander to and fro ;
Yet are we ever on the track Divine ;
The soul confesseth Thee, but sense is slow
To lean on aught but that which it may see ;
So hath it crowded up these Courts below
With dark and broken images of Thee ;
Lead Thou us forth upon Thy Mount, and show
Thy goodly patterns, whence these things of old
By Thee were fashioned ; One though manifold.
Glass Thou thy perfect likeness in the soul,
Show us Thy countenance, and we are WHOLE !

No one, I am quite certain, will regret that
I have made these liberal quotations. Apart
from their literary merit, they have a special
interest for the readers of "The Patience of
Hope," as more fully illustrating the writer's
personal experience and aspirations.

It has been suggested by a friend, that it is
barely possible that an objection may be urged
against the following treatise, as against all
books of a like character, that its tendency is
to isolate the individual from his race, and
to nourish an exclusive and purely selfish personal solicitude ; that its piety is self-absorb-
ent, and that it does not take sufficiently into
account active duties and charities, and the
love of the neighbor so strikingly illustrated
by the Divine Master in his life and teachings.
This objection, if valid, would be a fatal one.
For, of a truth, there can be no meaner type
of human selfishness than that afforded by
him who, unmindful of the world of sin and
suffering about him, occupies himself in the
pitiful business of saving his own soul in the
very spirit of the miser, watching over his
private hoard while his neighbors starve for lack
of bread. But surely the benevolent unrest,
the far-reaching sympathies and keen sensitive-
ness to the suffering of others, which so nobly

distinguish our present age, can have nothing to fear from a plea for personal holiness, patience, hope, and resignation to the Divine will. "The more piety, the more compassion," says Isaac Taylor; and this is true, if we understand by piety, not self-concentred asceticism, but the pure religion and undefiled which visits the widow and the fatherless, and yet keeps itself unspotted from the world,—which deals justly, loves mercy, and yet walks humbly before God. Self-scrutiny in the light of truth can do no harm to any one, least of all to the reformer and philanthropist. The spiritual warrior, like the young candidate for knighthood, may be none the worse for his preparatory ordeal of watching all night by his armor.

Tauler in mediæval times, and Woolman in the last century, are among the most earnest teachers of the inward life and spiritual nature of Christianity, yet both were distinguished for practical benevolence. They did not separate the two great commandments. Tauler strove with equal intensity of zeal to promote the temporal and the spiritual welfare of men. In the dark and evil time in which he lived, amidst the untold horrors of the "Black Plague," he illustrated by deeds of charity and mercy his doctrine of disinterested benevolence. Woolman's whole life was a nobler "Imitation of Christ" than that fervid rhapsody of monastic piety which bears the name.

How faithful, yet, withal, how full of kindness, were his rebukes of those who refused labor its just reward, and ground the faces of the poor? How deep and entire was his sympathy with overtasked and ill-paid laborers; with wet and ill-provided sailors, with poor wretches blaspheming in the mines, because oppression had made them mad; with the dyers plying their unhealthful trade to minister to luxury and pride; with the tenant wearing out his life in the service of a hard landlord; and with the slave sighing over his unrequited toil! What a significance there was in his vision of the "dull, gloomy mass" which appeared before him, darkening half the heavens, and which he was told was "human beings in as great misery as they could be and live; and he was mixed with them, and henceforth he might not consider himself a distinct and separate being"! His saintliness was wholly unconscious; he seems never to have thought himself any nearer to the tender heart of God than the most miserable sinner to whom his compassion extended. As he did not live, so neither did he die to himself. His prayer upon his death-bed was for others rather than himself; its beautiful humility and simple trust were marred by no sensual imagery of crowns and harps and golden streets, and personal beatific exaltations; but tender and touching concern for suffering humanity, relieved only by the thought of the paternity of God, and of his love and omnipotence, alone found utterance in ever-memorable words.*

In view of the troubled state of the country, and the intense preoccupation of the public mind, I have had some hesitation in offering this volume to its publishers. But, on further reflection, it has seemed to me that it might supply a want felt by many among us; that, in the chaos of civil strife, and the shadow of mourning which rests over the land, the con-

---

* "O Lord, my God! the amazing horrors of darkness were gathered about me, and covered me all over, and I saw no way to go forth; *I felt the depth and extent of the misery of my fellow-creatures separated from the Divine harmony, and it was greater than I could bear, and I was crushed down under it; I lifted up my hand, I stretched out my arm, but there was none to help me;* I looked round about, and was amazed. In the depths of misery, O Lord, *I remembered that Thou art omnipotent; that I had called thee Father;* and I felt that I loved thee; and I was made quiet in my will, and waited for deliverance from thee. Thou hadst pity upon me, when no man could help me; I saw that meekness under suffering was showed to us in the most affecting example of thy Son; and thou taught me to follow him, and I said, 'Thy will, O Father, be done!'"

templation of " things unseen which are eternal " might not be unwelcome; that, when the
foundations of human confidence are shaken,
and the trust in man proves vain, there might
be glad listeners to a voice, calling from the
outward and the temporal, to the inward and
the spiritual; from the troubles and perplexities
of time, to the eternal quietness which God
giveth. I cannot but believe that, in the heat
and glare through which we are passing, this
book will not invite in vain to the calm, sweet
shadows of holy meditation, grateful as the
green wings of the bird to Thalaba in the
desert; and thus afford something of consolation to the bereaved, and of strength to the
weary. For surely never was the " Patience
of Hope " more needed; never was the inner
sanctuary of prayer more desirable; never was
a steadfast faith in the Divine goodness more
indispensable, nor lessons of self-sacrifice and
renunciation, and that cheerful acceptance of
known duty which shifts not its proper respon-
sibility upon others, nor asks for " peace in
its day " at the expense of purity and justice,
more timely than now, when the solemn words
of ancient prophecy are as applicable to our
own country as to that of the degenerate Jew, —
" Thine own wickedness shall correct thee, and

thy backsliding reprove thee; know, therefore, it is an evil thing, and bitter, that thou hast forsaken the Lord, and that my fear is not in thee," — when " His way is in the deep, in clouds, and in thick darkness," and the hand heavy upon us which shall "turn and overturn until he whose right it is shall reign," — until, not without rending agony, the evil plant which our Heavenly Father hath not planted, whose roots have wound themselves about altar and hearthstone, and whose branches, like the tree Al-Accoub in Moslem fable, bear the accursed fruit of oppression, rebellion, and all imaginable crime, shall be torn up and destroyed forever.

J. G. W.

Amesbury, 1st 6th mo., 1862.

PART FIRST.

"He shall grow up as a tender plant,
As a root out of dry ground."

ISAIAH liii. 2.

The Patience of Hope.

PART I.

IN Jesus Christ all contradictions are reconciled ; yet in Him, also, and in all that is connected with his person and office, we are met by a strange contradiction, — a clashing of opposing attributes. " Who is this that cometh from Edom, with dyed garments from Bozrah, glorious in his apparel, travelling in the greatness of his strength ? He who hath trodden down the people in his wrath, and trampled upon them in his fury." Is this one with Him the Man of sorrows and of humiliation, of silence and long-suffering, despised of men and rejected, giving his back to the smiters, and his cheeks to them that plucked off the hair ? Is this Lord to whom the Lord hath spoken, " Sit thou on my right hand, until I make thine enemies thy footstool," Him concerning whom God speaks thus comfortably unto Zion, " Behold, thy King cometh, meek, having salvation, lowly, riding upon an ass, and a colt the foal of an ass "? is He, the upholder of the bruised reed, one with Him who shall bruise the nations with a rod of iron, and dash them in pieces like a potter's vessel? is the Interceder one with the Avenger? the Lamb that taketh away the sins of the world, one with Him whose wrath a guilty world shall not be able to abide ?

" Kiss the Son, lest he be angry." Can we wonder that some among the Jews should have imagined there would be two Messiahs, — the suffering one and the triumphant? And what is the Incarnation, but the fulfilment of these mighty, yet contending predictions? What is the life of our Lord and Saviour upon earth but the conflict of glory and humiliation? " The birth of Jesus Christ was on this wise " : glorious in fact, yet of ambiguous circumstance ; of kingly descent, yet lowly parentage ; born in the appointed city, yet called a Nazarene ; cradled in a manger, yet worshipped even there by sage and monarch ; dying a death of ignominy, yet even upon the Cross, in Hebrew and Greek and Latin, — the three living, ruling tongues of time, — proclaimed to be a King and a Saviour. " *This is Jesus* " ; possessed through life of

boundless resources, and exerting them on be-
half of others, yet himself submitting to the
ordinary conditions of the Humanity he had
taken upon him; hungering, thirsting, wearied,
in all things choosing to be made like unto his
brethren; Lord of nature and of time, yet waiting upon the restraints they impose; overcoming death, yet obedient to that which he over-
came. " He saved others, himself he cannot
save."

And as with the Master, so with them that
are of his Household. The history of the
Christian Church is a hieroglyph or picture-
writing, to which the life of Jesus Christ on
earth is as it were the Rosetta stone, making,
when once mastered, all the rest plain. The
present aspect of the Church, its past history,
the records of individual Christian experience,
offer us many sorrowful problems; but how
was it in the days when the Word was made
flesh and dwelt among us, and man *beheld* God's
glory, full of grace and truth? Was there not
even then something which corresponds with
what we now see and feel? — the final and
absolute contending with the temporal and
accidental, and often apparently overcome by
them; lofty principles out of harmony with
the things which surround them, — delay, vicis-

situde, incompleteness, — " the something still which prompts the eternal sigh." Is there not now in Christ something which corresponds with what we trace in the Gospel narrative ; something, I say, *which disappoints an apparently reasonable hope* like that of the devout * Jews for the temporal Messiah ; disappoints it to fulfil it far more gloriously, more completely, yet in a way that contradicts our natural expectations. Even then, as now, did Christ delay, withdraw, even hide himself from those that loved and followed him, " a deceiver, and yet true."

The history of Divine grace in the heart and in the world is illustrated by the book which St. John received from the angel, sweet to the taste, bitter in the working. Is it the Jew only who looks in Christ for the temporal deliverer, the restorer of paths to dwell in, the bringer again, like David, of all that the enemy hath carried away ? What finder of Jesus is there who has not in his first joy exclaimed, with St. Andrew, " We have found the Messias, that is the Christ " ? What follower of Jesus is there who does not learn, as did those first brethren, that " He must be followed to prison and to death " ?

* It is difficult, perhaps, for a Christian to place himself at the point of view they occupied so as to see *how* reasonable this hope was.

When Jesus says to his disciples, " In the world ye shall have tribulation," he speaks from insight rather than foresight ; as one who, knowing what was the heart of man, sees in himself the bringer of a sword within it, that shall never leave it until all things concerning him are fulfilled.

Let us consider this, — that when Christ took our nature upon him, *he took it as it was ;* he did not re-create before assuming it, but assumed it in order to its re-creation, so that, being found in fashion as a man, he brought himself into connection, yet into collision, with weakness, with error, with decay, *with all that belongs to man.* The conflict of Christianity is the harder because it is civil ; it has allied itself with that against which it must contend to the death, or be itself overcome of it. Hence its fierce collisions, its sorrowful victories ; hence too its still more sad, more fatal compromises, its unholy, unhallowing alliances, " the Woman sitting upon the Beast," *—the compact between the Church and the World, at the sight of which he who had learnt so many secrets from his beloved Master, yet " wondered with great admiration." And if the world itself is a field too narrow for the meeting-shock of such antagonists as grace

* See Williams on the *Apocalypse.*

and nature, how fares it in the conflict of which
all that passes in the outward Church is but the
history "writ large"; when these two, con-
trary the one to the other, meet and wrestle
within the heart as those who contend, not for
mastery, but for life itself? Woe, in this battle,
to the vanquished! woe also to the victor!
" For every battle of the warrior is with confused noise, and garments rolled in blood, but
this shall be with burning and fuel of fire."

Ellis tells us that during his stay in Madagas-
car he was visited by a native of rank, himself
friendly to Christianity, and who had suffered
deeply in his family relations in the persecution
through which, as through a fiery and bloody
dawn, its light so lately broke upon that island.
This man looked at the brother missionaries
long and earnestly, when, after almost mechani-
cally giving them his hands, there came over
his countenance, Ellis says, " an expression such
as I have never witnessed in any human being;
an intensity of feeling, neither ecstasy nor terror,
but an apparent blending of both; while during
the whole interview, which was long, there was
a *strange uneasiness* mingled with *an evident
satisfaction.*" Was there not here, even in the
twilight of faith and reason, a recognition of
Christ and of all that he comes to work? an

intuition in this half-enlightened, half-instructed
soul of what remains long hidden from Christ's
wise and prudent ones, — the stern necessity of
the Christian covenant, that Christ in his members, as once aforetime in his human person,
should suffer *many things* before he can enter
into his glory? It is hard for Humanity to receive this lesson, to accept this inevitable condition of its initiation into its true life, — *the laying
down of that very life, that we may receive it again
in Christ.* Hard for us, as it was for the first
disciples, even with Christ our Master going
" before us " on the foreseen path, to understand
him when he speaks of suffering, of humilation,
of death itself, shortly to be accomplished. Here
too, upon the way, will there be reasonings,
surmisings, something too within the heart
which, with the ardent spirit of St. Peter, will
resist, even rebuke the teaching of its beloved
Lord ; which will say unto him, " Be this far
from Thee." For what is this which Christ
demands from his disciple? *Even that which he
himself gave.* "Sacrifice and meat-offering thou
wouldest not, neither hadst pleasure therein."
The idea of propitiation, or the giving up of
something which we hold least precious in order
that we may retain that which we prize most of
all, upon which the sacrifices under the old law

and those of all natural religions are founded,
finds no place in the Christian Covenant.   For
to confirm this between God and man, *the most
precious thing of all was offered, and was accepted;* " He taketh away the first, that he may
establish the second."

And thus it is necessary that this Man also
should have something to offer.   The need of
sacrifice is not taken away, only its nature is
changed, exalted, deepened; and mild as is the
genius of the New Dispensation, its knife goes
closer to the heart than that of the elder one,
which we are accustomed to think of as so stern
and exacting.   Behold the goodness and severity of Christ!   " Skin for skin," saith Job of
old; " all that a man hath will he give for his
life."   And it is this very life which Christ
asks us to lay down for him; this life of which
he tells us, that he who loveth it shall lose it,
and he who loseth it for his sake, shall keep it
unto life eternal.

And when we speak in a spiritual sense of
Life, the laying it down and taking it again, we
speak not of mere existence, but of that which
is to every one of us the root by which we hold;
that which is to each individual heart confessed-
ly " no vain thing, for it is our life."   Take it
away, and all beside is gone; "for in the blood

is the life"; in the affections, in the energies
which send their sap through the whole think-
ing, feeling being. And it is to the root of *this*
tree of man's life, wrapped round with its most
intimate fibres, — even this, be it what it may,
for which we would give, for which we would
forego, all the world beside, — *the will of man*,
— that the axe of Christ is laid.

The disciple must be as his master, the servant as his lord. Why was the sacrifice of
Christ's death so pre-eminently meritorious, so
infinitely prevailing with God? why do the
sacred writers attribute an efficacy to it which
it was impossible that the sufferings of unconscious though innocent victims could possess?
Because, to say nothing of the intrinsic value of
this sacrifice, it was, above all others that have
been ever offered, a free, conscious, and willing one. The Man Christ Jesus was, of all
created beings, — as far as we know their history, — the only one who chose his own destiny,
who foreknew and accepted its full conditions;
who saw a great need, and responded to it,
"Lo! I come." " My leave," said the acute
Frenchwoman, " was not asked before I came
into the world," — a saying in which all that
the human heart can urge against God and his
appointments lies hid. Why should I be called

upon to endure, to forego so much? Had the
choice been permitted me, I might possibly have
declined it. *Our Saviour's leave was asked.* His
fulfilment of his Father's will was voluntary ; he
saw the end from the beginning; *saw it even in
the beginning*, and walked onwards to that end,
seeing his own destiny and feeling his own freedom. " I have power," he says, " to lay down
my life, and I have power to take it again."

But how is Christ's follower to obtain this
freedom? How is this great transfer, lying at
the very heart of our spiritual life, the exchange
of our own will for a better one, to be effected
for a being like Man, impelled alike by the
weakness and the strength of his whole nature
to cleave unto the dust from whence he was
at first taken? At this point we must pause a
moment, feeling that our subject has drawn us
into a desolate, even awful region, where, like
the traveller high up among the mountains, we
would fain hold the breath and hurry onwards,
lest a word too lightly spoken should bring down
the impending avalanche. For all thoughts that
lead us from the circumference of faith to its
centre draw us insensibly, and with a force that
becomes irresistible the nearer we approach that
centre, to the sacrifice of the death of Christ.
Motus rerum est rapidus extra locum, placidus

in loco. There is no rest for the soul of the
believer till it settles forever on this magnet.
No rest; I would say, also, no progress for the
soul until it receives within it this great Motive
Power; receives it not only as a fulfilled fact,
but accepts it in its boundless consequences, and
recognizes as first among them that of its own
"baptism unto his death." The disciple is not
above his master, neither is the servant above
his Lord; *nevertheless, every one that is perfect
shall be as his master.* O blessed saying! O
promise like unto that made to the two chosen
disciples, "Ye shall indeed drink of my cup";
and what if our Lord's cup should prove to be
the cup of vinegar mingled with gall, it is none
the less the cup of blessing and of full, unre-
served communion. "Kiss me with the kisses
of thy mouth, for thy love is better than wine."

And it is our personal initiation into this
mystery of sacrifice which is, as regards the life
which is in Christ Jesus, its true sacrament,
enabling the soul to pass into real and intimate
communion with him. Christ our Passover has
been long slain for us; but how do his people,
for the most part, keep the feast? *By way of
commemoration only.*

But it is they who eat of the sacrifices, and
they only, who are partakers of the Altar. It

is not enough that we show forth our Lord's
death until his coming again; to draw out the
depths of this great act of love, we must so
unite ourselves to it as to learn what St. Paul
meant when he spoke of filling up that which
was behind of the sufferings of Christ. It is the
bearing of the cross, the sharing of the passion,
that enables the believer to meet and understand
his Lord; "for we being many, are one Body,"
and without participation there can be no communion.

All that are in Christ must be made to drink
into one Spirit, yet often and often perhaps must
He return and ask his chosen ones, "Are ye
able to drink of my cup?" before that free, calm
answer can be given, "We are able"; and
many offerings must be laid upon his altar with
tears and weeping before the *sacrifices of joy* are
brought there. For as Christ was made like
unto us, we must *be made like unto him*, even at
the cost of much that is grievous to natural feeling. His coming within the soul is the bringing in of a new order; and when was there a
painless transition, a bloodless revolution? It
gives a new aim to the will of man; it sets a
fresh goal before his affections, and one ofttimes to be reached only by passing over the
dead body of all that made up their former life.

" Who will lead me into the strong city? who will bring me into Edom?"   Before Christ can gain the citadel of Man's will and affections, many pleasant places must be laid waste before him, many fair and flourishing outworks be brought low.   These are hard sayings, and if they are met by the rejoinder, *Who* can bear them? the answer is already written, *They to whom they are addressed by Christ, and they only.* " He who forsaketh not all that he hath, cannot be my disciple."   Christ does not say he cannot be my servant, does not say he cannot be my son, but he cannot be my disciple.   There are many gains, many losses in Christ, over and above that great, inappreciable loss of the salvation of the soul in him.   This final aim may be attained, and yet the hearers who, for love of a great or of a small possession, depart upon that saying, " Sell that thou hast, and follow me," may have abundant reason for going away sorrowful.   We are made poor by what we miss, as well as by what we lose; * a little more patience,

---

* You say in one of your letters, "I feel a solemn pathos in the lament which the Lord takes up over the defection of his people: ' O that my people had hearkened unto me, that Israel had walked in my ways! I should soon have subdued their enemies, and turned my hand against their adversaries'; and after this follows, ' I should have fed them with the finest wheat flour, and with honey out of the stony rock should I have satisfied them.' And what, but for a like failure in perseverance might

a little more constancy, and to what might we not have attained! to what tender intimacy, to what satisfying communications, to what power, what rest, what freedom!

The more clearly we follow Christ, the more perseveringly do certain truths present themselves to us, — truths with which we commune, but dare not for a while receive in their full import, because we know they would lead us whither we would not. Yet they come again and again, offering themselves to us, like the Sibyl of old, each time under harder conditions, till at last we accept them on their own terms. A Christian may love his Master truly, and be yet unprepared to follow him whithersoever he goeth. How can two walk in a way unless they be agreed? and the enmity between Christ and nature is not yet so wholly slain but that there may be on the believer's part conscious shrinkings and reservations: he knows that it would be hard to take this thing up; hard, perhaps impossible, to let this thing go, even at the com-

have been *our* portion, 'the finest of the wheat, and honey out of the rock,' and *that Rock*, St. Paul tells us, *was Christ*. To hearken diligently unto him, to walk in his ways, is plainly pointed out as the means through which we first obtain victory over our spiritual enemies, and then arrive at the feast of good things, prepared for those only who have come thus far. 'I will bring them into my banqueting-house, where my banner over them shall be love.' " — J. E. B.

mand of Christ himself. This crisis of spiritual
life, full of pain and perplexity, is one with
which our Saviour may deeply sympathize, for
he knoweth what is in Man; yet it is none the
less a temper which "is not worthy of Him."
He does not trust himself to a divided heart, and
of this the owner of such a heart is well aware.
So that there arises within it a secret craving for
whatever may detach and loosen these bonds,
from which no effort of its own can free it, —
a desire like that which St. Paul so fervently
expresses *for the fellowship of his Lord's sufferings, the conformity to his Lord's death,* so that
by any means it may attain to spiritual resurrection with him. There comes a moment in
which the soul, awaking up into the sense of
the deep antagonism between grace and nature,
will exclaim, as seeing no other way of deliverance, "Let us go *unto Him,* that we may also
die with him"; let us know that we live in
Christ, if it be through being sharers in his pain.

"They were all baptized in the cloud and in
the sea"; this is the register of all Christ's
chosen ones, the pledge of their initiation into
that covenant "whose promises, whose rewards,
whose very beatitudes are sufferings." *Why*
does St. Paul so rejoice,* so delight himself in

* Note A.

weakness, in persecution, in affliction, but because he knows that *without these* he can attain
to no close intimacy with his beloved Lord?
And if this be a sore lesson, is it not one for
which the heart may be in some degree prepared, even by its own natural experience?   Do
not trials and sorrows (also, it is true, deep joys)
shared between two friends, partings, dangers,
above all, the having stood together in the presence of death, deepen the channel of our affection in deepening that of our existence?   Are
not such moments as it were sacramental, bringing us nearer each other in bringing us nearer
God, from whom the poor unrealities of time,
unworthy of us as they are of Him, too much
divide us?   It is often through some keen, even
desolating shock, the blasting of the breath of
God's chiding, that the deep foundations of our
nature are first discovered to us.   When the
veil of the temple, even this poor worn garment
of our Humanity, is rent from the top to the
bottom, we catch glimpses of the inner glory:
the rocks are riven, the graves open, they who
have long slept in the dust come forth, and
reveal to us awful and tender secrets, of which
otherwise we should have known nothing.
" They who love," as says St. Chrysostom, "if
it be but man, not God," will know what I

mean, when I speak of joys springing out of
the very heart of anguish, and holding to it
by a common and inseparable life; will understand how it comes that the pale flowers which
thrust themselves out of the ruins of hope, of
endeavor, of affection, — yes, even out of the
mournful wreck of intellect itself, — should
breathe out a deep and intimate fragrance, such
as the broad wealth of air and sunshine never
yet gave, —

> " For in things
> That move past utterance, tears ope all their springs,
> *Nor are there in the powers that all life bears*
> *More true interpreters of all than tears.*"

It needs but a little consideration to perceive
that devotion, self-sacrifice, all the higher moods
and energies even of natural feeling, are only
possible to seasons of adversity. " Deep calleth
unto deep." We need not look far into Man's
nature to see that its true wealth does not lie
so near the surface, but that the smooth, grassy
levels of prosperity hide riches such as only a
shock can develop. The history of both nations
and churches shows us how the very strain and
pressure of calamity can force up social existence
to an otherwise unimaginable height of nobleness ; but we must look yet deeper than this,
to understand the strange affinity which Christianity has at all times betrayed with whatever

is most contradictory to natural feeling, making
it to choose pain and weakness and infirmity as
its natural soil and climate.   And here experience, rather than reason, must be our guide ; for
what is there in pain, considered in itself, that is
purifying, far less ennobling ?   Its connection
with all that is most precious to Christian life
is incidental rather than inherent, and is to be
traced to that deep original wound of our nature
which has set the ideals of Christ and Humanity
so far apart, that the wealth of the one can only
be attained through the minishing of the other.
If the house of David is to wax stronger, the
house of Saul must wax weaker from day to day.
And hence it is that every fuller development
of Christ's spirit within man *necessarily* takes a
self-subduing character, making asceticism under
one form or other inseparable from the true
Christian life.   For the glory of the terrestrial is
one, the glory of the celestial is another.   The
triumph of Nature lies in the carrying out of
its own will, in identification with some great
object, in adhesion to some lofty aim.   The
triumph of Christ is placed in the subjugation
of that very will, in acquiescence, in disen-
tanglement; in the stretching forth of the
hands, so that another may gird us and carry
us whither we would not.*

* Note B.

The character which Christ forms within the heart is one at variance with our ideas of natural greatness; His rule opposes itself as much to the higher as to the lower instincts of nature. And that this should have been most clearly seen by thinkers looking at Christianity from without, ought not to make us careless of the truths they disclose; for intellectual and spiritual contemplation alike lead up to clear, calm summits, and upon them are strange meetings undreamt of by the dwellers in the valleys and the plains below. The keen intuition of the Thinker places him in possession of truths which the lowly Christian has learned upon his knees; and though these two may distrust and be mutually repelled from each other, they have none the less a common standing-ground, —

"Their speech is one, their witnesses agree."

The sober Christian may possibly feel a shock in finding Novalis describe his faith as a foe " to art, to science, even to enjoyment"; yet does not his own daily experience prove that the holding of the one thing needful involves the letting go of many things lovely and desirable, and that in thought, as well as in action, he must go on " ever narrowing his way, *avoiding much*"?*   And this, not because his intellect

* W. B. Scott.

is darkened to perceive beauty and excellence,
or his affections dulled to embrace them, but
because human life and human capacity are
bounded things ; the heart can be devoted but
to *one* object, and the winning of the great
prizes of earthly endeavor asks for an intensity
of purpose, which in the Christian has found
another centre.

And more than this, the rule of Christ is not
only exclusive but restrictive, and though it
would carry us among too wide and distant
fields to enter upon this subject as it deserves,
we need not look far into either literature or art
to see to how many of their happiest energies
this rule opposes itself.   Their spirit is a free
spirit, impatient of any yoke.   How much, for
instance, of the greatness of Shakespeare and
Goethe consists in a wide Naturalism, which,
as it were, finds room within it for all things,
not only depicting them, but in some measure
delighting in them, *as they are.*   Could this
genial abandonment coexist with a deepened
moral consciousness, far less, surely, with the
simplicity and severity of Christ ?

Again : to a person who has seen in Christianity a certain engaging moral and social aspect, and has not looked into it much deeper,
what Goethe says of it as being " founded upon

the reverence for that which is beneath us, the
veneration of the hated, the contradictory, and
the avoided," will appear perverse and one-
sided. Yet not so, surely, to him who has
been accustomed to recognize his Lord's features
in those of the forlorn, the ignorant, and the despised, — to him who has found that the print of
his Master's footsteps, if tracked with any degree
of faithfulness, will carry his own far out of the
path of pleasure and distinction, and leave him
amid scenes and among objects in which, save
for this powerful attraction, he would have found
nothing to delight in or to desire. For Christianity, though it may at certain periods and
in certain persons reveal itself under a splendid
and engaging aspect, so as to command the
homage * of the world with which it is at variance, remains true to its first conditions, beginning at Bethlehem, "small among the cities of
Judah," and ending upon Calvary between the
two thieves. Whenever it has been joined, as it
has been joined so often, with the pomp and
riches and glory of this world, this has been but
a State-alliance, from which its heart has fled, to
the cell of the lonely monk, to the workshop of
the humble artisan, to some little band of perse-
cuted men, — to such as, whether solitary or in
families, —

3 *   * Note C.

"Loving Jesus for his own sake,"

have been content for his sake to be men wondered at.*   How many of the sparks at which great fires have been kindled, even now enlightening and warming the world, have been struck from the hearts and brains of men counted fools and fanatics in their own generation!   Christ is favorable to the simple and needy.   When we look into His kingdom, we see that many of its mightiest enterprises, now ripening to evident perfection, have been begun by a few gathered together in his name, and these few, perhaps, neither wise nor rich nor noble.   Yet even now, as during our Lord's life on earth, all the lowliness of his aspect does not conceal the loftiness of his claims, nor blind the world to the

---

* " He who far off beholds another dancing,
   Even he who dances best, and all the time
   Hears not the music that he dances to,
   Thinks him a madman, apprehending not
   The law which moves his else eccentric motion;
   So he that 's in himself insensible
   Of love's sweet influence misjudges him
   Who moves according to love's melody.
   And knowing not that all these sighs and tears,
   Ejaculations and impatiences,
   Are necessary changes of a measure
   Which the divine musician plays, may call
   The lover crazy, which he would not do,
   Did he within his own heart hear the tune
   Played by the great musician of the world."
                    CALDERON, *translated by* FITZGERALD.

fact that these are the claims of one who, coming in to sojourn, has made himself *altogether*
a ruler and a judge over it. "Whom makest
thou thyself?" it will still ask. And this question will be followed by a demand, prompted by
kindred enmity, "Why makest thou us to
doubt? if thou be the Christ, show thyself
openly."

And there is much, truly, in the condition of
the Church since our Saviour left it to remind
us of the plant Linnæus speaks of, — perfect in
its structure, yet showing neither fruit nor blossom above the earth, though it puts forth many
beneath it, blanched from the darkness of their
life. "It doth not yet appear what we shall
be." Humanity, even at the voice of Christ,
comes forth bound hand and foot with grave-
clothes, and as one that hath been dead four
days. Therefore we need not wonder if in such
a resurrection there should be paroxysms; if
there should be in every great awakening unto
Christ something to give room for the scoffings
of the profane, the doubts and surmisings of the
prudent. Christ does not at once remove the
enmity which he finds. He must first bind the
strong man; and before the strength of nature
is subdued and disciplined to carry out the
behests of grace, there is a struggle, — revealing

itself among the poor of Christ's flock, unused to restrain or analyze their own emotions, in forms which may appear strange and exceptionable, but from which, under one form or another, none in whose spirit Christ lives can escape. For the heart and the world, until renewed after His likeness, are still heathen in all but in name; exorcism must precede baptism, and the baptism from our Lord's hand is that wherewith he himself was baptized, — *signed with the sign of the cross.**

And while these thoughts throw an incidental light upon much that is mysterious in our spiritual life, they draw us to the consideration of that deeper mystery which underlies it all, — the structure, the schematism of our faith, which reveals itself through the fair and often smiling surface of Christianity as the gray rock in some mountain district crowns every summit, and thrusts itself even through the sheep-covered slopes, in keen contrast with their peace and verdure. When man finds that, if he would do God's will, however imperfectly, he must offer up this continual sacrifice, *the sacrifice of his own*

---

* Adalbert, the martyred apostle of Prussia, slain by the fierce Wends, stretched forth both his arms in dying, saying, " Jesus, receive thou me," and fell with his face to the ground in the form of a crucifix, thus, Carlyle says, setting his mark upon that heathen country.

will, his thoughts are irresistibly carried to rest upon that One offering up of a higher than any human will,* by which Christ has perfected forever them that are sanctified. The more deeply we feel the existing contradiction between God's will and that of his creature, the deeper becomes our sense of the need of somewhat to take it away, so that the heart draws near to a truth unapproachable by the intellect, — *the necessary death of Christ.* All things in nature, as well as all things in grace, point to a Redeemer. Nature struggles, but cannot speak ; she remains in bondage with her children, dumb like them, and beautiful. Humanity has found a voice ; but where, save for Christ, would she find an answer ? She has showed him of her wound, her grievous, incurable hurt; and how has he consoled her ? Even by showing her His, — " Reach hither thy hand, and thrust it into my side."

And as the law was our schoolmaster to bring us to Christ, so does our daily experience become a school, teaching us the same deep lesson which the book of the Old Testament unfolds. The events of human life, and the great facts which revelation discloses, cast reciprocal light upon each other, so that the believer's course

* See Hebrews x. 10.

as he advances is ever instructing him, like the
Earlier Dispensation, through hint and sign and
shadow, in the mysteries on which all the visible
dealings of God are grounded.

We begin to see that the whole teaching of
the human race by God is based, like the prophetic songs of the Old Covenant, upon a gigantic parallelism ; * that as the Type is not a mere
Sign, but has a *real* † *though unseen* connection
with the fact it shadows forth, so has that fact
also its correlative lying deep in the nature of
God and man, and testifying to the essential
unity of those natures.   And as through the
awful imagery which, under the rites and cere-
monies of the Old Dispensation, prefigured the
stupendous event of Redemption, we discern a
mighty underworking which threw these figures
of sacrifice and atonement to the surface, *and
could not have appeared in any other ;* so, as our
Christian consciousness deepens, do the things

* Note D.

† Differing in this from a symbol, which, being merely an *idea
shown*, a species of shorthand or figure-writing, need possess, it is
obvious, no other than an arbitrary connection with the thing it
stands for. A rose, for instance, once adopted, for whatever
reason, as the emblem of secrecy, always conveys that idea to
the mind which, in the absence of any natural association between the two things, has once received them in connection.
But it is far otherwise with a Type, which is, as Warburton
says, "a prophecy in action, one in nature with that which it
represents." — See on this subject the *Divine Legation*, 9th Book.

with which we are daily conversant take up a
mute significance; so does all in life, that once
appeared without bearing on our higher desti-
nies, begin to arrange itself in the pattern
of heavenly things, "the pattern showed us in
the mount."

And though the great events of Incarnation
and Redemption, casting light upon all that had
gone before them, *need themselves,** according
to Gaussen's fine saying, *to be illumined by a
light not yet risen*, though the Dispensation of
glory has yet to illustrate that of grace, it is in
the heart that the day-star must now arise.

And in every believing heart, the gradual
turning of that heart to Christ casts as it were
an oblique light on the sacred revelations of
Scripture, by awakening within it the sense of
sin, the need of expiation, and the want of a
better righteousness than our own to meet a
standard which even man, when once renewed
in aim and feeling, consciously aspires to. So
that the heart accepts Christ because it needs
him, even while the mind may be unable to
receive him fully, because the orbit of this Star
is so extended as to carry beyond it the sphere
of human intelligence. "For to this end Jesus
Christ both died and suffered, and rose again,

* Note E.

that he might be Lord both of the living and
the dead." We know not upon how many
points Redemption touches ; what unseen
worlds, what unborn generations, what unde-
veloped forms of being it embraces. We know
not to what Warfare, to what Accomplishment, our Lord referred when he spoke those
words, "It is finished." We know not, in short,
as Butler says, what in the works and counsels of God are ends, and what means to a further end, or how what appears to us as final
may be initial with Him. But we see enough
around us, and within us, to show that it was
necessary that Christ should suffer many things,
and after that enter into his glory; enough to
learn that we shall find no higher thing above,
shall pierce to no deeper thing below, than the
Cross and its solemn and tender teachings. If
we would climb up into heaven, it is there ; if
we would go down into hell, it is there also.
He alone among men who has clasped this great
mystery of grief and love to his bosom sees, if it
be as yet but through a glass darkly, how pain
and love, yes, joy also, *all things that have a
living root in humanity* come to bloom under its
shadow. And how love that cannot die, and
faith that grows to certainty, and hope that
maketh not ashamed, root themselves about it,

with all fair things that wither in life, and noble things for which it has no room. " I took," said Luther, " for the symbol of my theology, a seal on which I had engraven a cross with a heart in its centre; the cross is black, to indicate the sorrows, even unto death, through which the Christian must pass, *but the heart preserves its natural color*, for the cross does not extinguish nature, it does not kill, but gives life. *Justus fide vivet, sed fide crucifixi.* The heart is placed in the midst of a white rose, which signifies the joy, peace, and consolation that faith gives; *but the rose is white, and not red*, because it is not the joy and peace of the world, but that of spirits."

" Whoso is wise will ponder these things, and he shall understand the loving-
kindness of the
Lord."

Show me more love, my dearest Lord,
  O, turn away thy clouded face!
Give me some secret look or word
  That may betoken love and grace;
No day or time is black to me
But that wherein I see not Thee;
Show me more love; *a clouded face*
  Strikes deeper than an angry blow.
Love me and kill me by thy grace,
  I shall not much bewail my woe.
          But even to be
  In heaven unloved of Thee
  Were hell in heaven for to see;
Then hear my cry, and help afford;
Show me more love, my dearest Lord.

Show me more love, my dearest Lord,
  I cannot think, nor speak, nor pray;
Thy work stands still; my strength is stored
  In Thee alone; O come away!
Show me thy beauties, *call them mine,*
My heart and tongue will soon be thine.
Show me more love, or if my heart
  Too common be for such a guest,
Let thy good Spirit by its art
  Make entry and put out the rest.
          For 't is thy nest;
  Then he 's of heaven possest
  That heaven hath in his breast.
Then hear my cry, and help afford;
Show me more love, my dearest Lord!

Part Second.

"And Joseph knew his brethren,
But they knew not him."

GEN. xlii. 8.

PART II.

WHEN the Past and the Future cheat us, it is through a charm to which we consciously abandon ourselves: we know how much the landscape gains in each case from the atmosphere through which we view it. But the Present is the true deceiver; its clear, cold daylight hides much, in appearing to conceal nothing from us, for it is possible to look at things so closely as not to see what they really are. We catch the mean detail; we miss the grand, comprehensive outline. We must stand farther off, so that we may see the whole. "When the great Athanasius lived on earth," says Pascal, "he did not appear in the light in which we now regard him; he was only a man called Athanasius." Yet was the great Athanasius *the true Athanasius*. And even thus greatness ever stands among us, as "one whom we know not"; know not, even because we think we know it so well.

And as of individuals, so of ages. It seems hard to be generous, not easy even to be just, to the times upon which our lot is cast. The very expression " our present day " conveys with it somewhat of disparagement, implying a contrast with other ages in whose very silence we find an eloquence rebuking the clamor that surrounds us. Yet much that we now look upon as prosaic, and perhaps decry as unreal, if read as history, would enchain our imaginations ; if spoken as prophecy, would stir our very souls. Future chroniclers will make it their wisdom to decipher the Runes we are now dinting, and will understand their import better than we who leave them on the rock.

Ours is a sober enthusiasm, patient because it is so strong. A Work is set before the day we live in, a Necessity is laid upon it ; it sees and accepts its calling, content to labor in the thick smoke, and weary itself among the very fires of speculation. Let but our age apprehend a cause, or an idea, as worthy of its devotion, and it will not fail to be furnished with apostles, with confessors, yes, if need be, with martyrs ; so strong is the passion of its onward march, so steadfast the ardor of its perseverance. And thus in how many a fair and still extending region of human thought and labor we have already arrived

" At the winning and the holding of a prize,
    The hope of which would have been once deemed madness."

But with our spiritual and moral conquests
it has surely fared less brightly ; here, among
many leaders, we have as yet no Columbus,
" the naked pilot, promiser of kingdoms," be-
stowing more than he had promised ; no prophets, such as science has been blessed with, who
have lived to see the wonder of their dream
surpassed by its sober interpretation.   Yet ours
is none the less an age of generous experi-
ments, of failures more noble than the successes
to which the world decrees a Triumph.   How
many laborers are now among us, literally water-
ing God's garden with their foot ! — a holy and
blessed work ; but one in which we must not
forget that the country in which our work lies
is *a land rich in itself*, full of fountains and
depths springing out of its own hills and valleys,
" a land that drinketh water of the rain of
heaven."   You say to me in one of your letters,
" We hear so much around us of doings, so
much of Christian exertion and charitable endeavor, that in witnessing the comparatively
small result of much devoted labor, I have been
led to believe that we work too much upon the
surface.   The waters of life lie below it, and
few pierce deep enough to unlock them for them-

selves or others. Our endless external reforms are, after all, only channels, too often dry ones, while every believer in whom his Lord's promise has been fulfilled, ' I will be to him a well of water, springing up into everlasting life,' is a fountain, hidden it may be to the eye, but discernible in the greenness and moisture that surround it."

We have more than enough of systems, of machinery, which, whether more or less perfect, will not go of itself. We may have done all that of ourselves we can do, and the moving spring may yet be wanting.* " *The spirit of the living creature in the wheels.*"

And just where our national dread of enthusiasm is the strongest, we have surely many enthusiasts among us ; soldiers who go upon a spiritual warfare at their own cost, and builders who expect with such materials as earth can furnish to reach even unto heaven. Yet God is a spirit, and Man is also a spirit, and all work that is done between God and Man must be done in the spirit, — must be wrought from the centre outwards. The life that lies at the circumference of its guiding idea lies there but in faint outline, feebly drawn, like the outermost ripple on disturbed waters. We are anxious to

* Ezekiel i. 19, 20; x. 16, 17.

spread the knowledge of God. This is *our work*, the end to which Christian exertion is chiefly directed, but before we can pursue it to any true result, God must also work a work within us, upon the deepening of which the extension of Christ's kingdom naturally, inevitably follows. For they who are rooted in the Lord will in him bud and blossom, and fill the face of the earth with fruit. All who have ever been strong for God, have been strong *in Him*, and have known too, as Samson did, where the secret of their strength lay, — in a dependence out of which they would have been consciously weak, and as other men. The Church has always borne witness to this truth; her every prayer and confession proves that she has seen how it is that which binds her to her Lord, that strengthens her in him, so that the chains which are about her neck have become " an ornament of grace upon her head." But here, too, she may take a lesson where her Lord has sent her to look for it.

Even from this Generation. Full of faith and power in the resources of human energy, and in that faith and power working marvels, if it believed in God as firmly as it does in itself, the seed it would raise to serve Him would be of no degenerate stock, and the Church would

4

once more, as in the days of its youth, take up its ancient hero-song, sweeter than was ever earthly Saga. But are we as Christians what we are as men?

God has showed us earthly things, and we have believed. Man has taken his own measure, and found it "the measure of an angel." *
Human intelligence, once a bold guesser after unproven truth, has learned the extent of its own resources; hence its sure, yet extended aims, and hence its glorious acquisitions. Opinions with us are rooted and seeded things, able to raise up the life which they contain within them. We embrace facts, not abstractions; *we live as men in the reality of that which we speculatively accept as true.* But can we say this for ourselves as Christians? Have we believed when God has showed us heavenly things, or yet taken the measure of a man in Christ? Are we as conversant with the Second Adam as with the First; as familiar with the capabilities of the renewed spirit as with those of the living soul? The facts of revelation are accepted. The Gospel is made the basis of law and of society; it is a framework holding all together; a code, like the great Roman one, upon which the mediæval world kept its hold so long after

* E. B. Browning.

the power and spirit of the empire were but a tradition. . . . .

But how few among us are of it upholden. How few, fastening upon God through the awful relations it discloses, can say from the deep and ground of the heart, " O Lord, *by these* men live, and *in them* is the life of the Spirit." And thus a strange weariness overtakes us ; *

---

* I leave these words as they were written. Yet, since then, even within the last few years, a change has come, far more gradually than is generally supposed, over the climate of the Christian world; as if some mighty current, like the Gulf Stream, had set in, sending a warm breath across the universal Church, and breaking up the deadly ice of ages of unbelief and indifference. And though this change may be, and will be, accompanied with shocks and splittings, it is surely the prudent, not the *wise* Christian, who will on this account withdraw himself from its wide, soul-enlarging influence. For it is evident that this is not a work of extension only; in every community, and in every heart where God has already had a work, that work has been lately deepened. " The river of God is full of water." He has not only sent rain upon the dwellings in the wilderness, but caused it to descend into furrows long since drawn. Experienced Christians are the natural guides and comforters of those whose hearts have been but lately made soft with the drops of heaven; in every Pentecostal outpouring there is something to recall the deep unconscious truth of that saying, " These men are full of new wine "; and it is *their* part to see that the wine is not spilled, neither the bottles marred. And while it is easy to cavil at the phenomena connected more or less remotely with this change, the fact, *not to be affected by any of them*, remains, that a great moral and spiritual change is taking place at our very doors; that the poor among men are rejoicing in their Maker; that multitudes of people are at this very moment lifting up praying hearts, and this, for no temporal blessing, no sectarian end, but simply for the clearer

uneasy in ourselves, we do not find rest in God,
and become aware of a deep question, underly-
ing all the shallow ones that now vex the current of religious speculation. We feel, each
one of us for himself, that the point at issue is
still concerning " one Jesus," whether we shall
say with the world that he is dead, or with
Paul steadfastly affirm him to be alive, and still
the resurrection of the spiritually dead, the life
of them that believe. For human society is
even now, as in the days when the Gospel was
first preached, made up of Greeks enthralled by
outward sense, of Jews resting in an outward
law ; and out of the midst of these a people has

---

light of Christ's Cross, the fuller manifestation of His Presence.
" I will hear, saith the Lord; I will hear the heavens, *and they
shall hear the earth* "; the heart of man seems set upon attaining
to this closer correspondence with his Maker, set, too, upon ob-
taining it through the Man whom he hath sent. *They who seek
the Lord shall praise him.* On all sides there is a sound of abundance of rain; so that the Christian feels that, deep and many as
may be the trials yet in store for the Church, it has turned over,
perhaps forever, one leaf of sorrowful experience, *that of its long
ploughing in the cold,* each laborer apart, and uncommunicating.
The days of harvest are sultry and arduous, but the reapers work
in bands, and are cheered by many a song: —

> " ' Brother, take thy brothers with thee,'
> Speak the silver-winding brooklets
> To the mighty mountain torrent;
> ' Take us with thee to the ocean
> That with outstretched arms awaits us, —
> Oft, alas! in vain awaits us.

need to be yet more fully called, to find Him
who is the end of the law to every one that
believeth : " Christ the power of God, and
Christ the wisdom of God."

Even now, said St. John, speaking of his own
day, there are many Antichrists. Since then
there have been many forms of denial, sundry
kinds of spiritual death. Christ has long stood
in this world's judgment-hall, and suffered many
things from them that throng it. From age to
age false witnesses have risen up, laying to his
charge things that he knew not. He has heard
the defaming of the multitude, and borne in his
bosom the rebukes of many peoples long gath-

> For in sandy wastes we filter
> Drop by drop, until the sunbeams
> Drink our blood; until some hillock
> Locks us to a pool. O take us,
> Brother, with thee!' Then for answer
> Swells the Flood, and on its bosom
> Lifts its kindred, lifts and bears them
> In its rolling triumph down.
> Lands take Name, and cities Being
> From its ceaseless march; behind it
> Tower and turret rise; upon it
> Float the goodly ships of cedar,
> Fair, with many a flying pennon
> Waving witness to its pride.
>   *Bearing in its joyful tumult,*
>   *Bearing still its brothers with it,*
>   *These its treasures, these its children,*
>   *To the waiting Father's heart.*"

ered to the dust of silence. But the day of in-
solent derision is over, and it is after another
manner that we behold Christ rejected, and set
at naught by this generation. We are met,
comparatively speaking, by little direct opposition to revealed religion; its moral teaching is
respected; the sacred person of its Founder is
held in reverence; it is as a power that Christianity is denied.* Our age has nothing in common with the degrading scepticism of the past
century, which cast its scorn up to God through
the foul dishonoring of His image. We believe,
as I have said, in Man; and our noble and tender faith in Humanity is one which works by
love, showing itself in persevering and arduous
efforts after social amelioration. But here also
we may find a fulfilment of our Lord's saying, —

---

* The lightest leaf will show the way the wind is setting, and
I know not where we are met by a plainer expression of this
tacit, and in some degree respectful denial, than in the popular
literature of our day. Here we see a systematic ignoring of
Christianity, combined with a rather inconsistent exaltation of
the benevolent aspect peculiarly belonging to it. We find in such
writings many flowers to please us, but see that, as in a child's
garden, they are stuck into the ground by their stalks only, *and
have not grown where we now see them.* We know that even the
lily floating on the waters, the orchid hanging in the air, keeps a
tenacious yet unseen hold upon something beyond itself, without
which its nourishment and life would fail; and all this bloom and
verdure is suggestive of a root, possessing, it may be, no beauty
for which we should desire it, yet detached from which the leaf
of humanity will wither and its flower fade.

"I am come in my Father's name, and ye receive me not; another will come in his own
name, him shall ye receive." The prophets
who come in their own name, the apostles of
human development, of social progress, find a
willing hearing; but where is our recognition of
a divinely appointed agency? where is our faith
in that which hath appeared to man?

But because we believe in Man; because we
reason, if not always aright, of truth, of beauty,
of perfection, and are full of reverence, full of
pity for the nature in which we find ourselves so
fearfully and wonderfully fashioned; because our
age, with all its wants and errors, is still a loving, a believing, an essentially *human* age, there
shall yet come to pass concerning it the saying
which is written, "In that day shall A MAN be
more precious than gold, than the golden wedge
of Ophir." The heart of this age is in its right
place, and with that heart it may yet believe
unto righteousness, and escape the downward
path towards which so many of its intellectual
tendencies are dragging it. We have not yet
drawn forth the true bitterness of the fruit
whose mortal taste is already so plainly to be
discerned among us, or many a yet noble and
tender spirit would exclaim, "Let not the pit
shut her mouth upon me,"— Materialism, the

grave of all that is human, as well as of all
that is heavenly, within man. The heart craves
what the world would take from it; Man needs
what no system invented by man has yet promised, far less given, — a Comforter, an enlightening, guiding Spirit, wanting which he remains
a mockery even to himself, the sport of circumstance, a Samson blind and fettered in the hall
of the Philistines. "*The world knows but a
Creator, spirits claim a Father.*" And O that
we could see that He has already come forth to
meet us; that we could, even in this our day,
perceive the season of our heavenly visitation,
and see to what its rejection tends, — a moral
atheism, blotting out God from the region of
spiritual life, as surely as the denial of a Personal cause excludes Him from the visible
world.

"There is a Spirit in man," faithful to its instincts even when astray as to their true object;
it wanders often, yet feels through very sadness
and weariness how far it has got from home.
And hence come those utterances (of which you
tell me), strange prophetic voices, a groaning
and travail-pain of Humanity, which, even in the
hearts of those who reject revelation, testify to
its waiting for some great Redemption. If man
refuses the bread which came down from heav-

en, never was it so hard for him to live "by
bread alone" as now.   His very wealth and increase has brought with it a sense of poverty, —
because he has become rich, and increased in
goods, he knows, as he did not before, that he is
wretched, and miserable, and blind, and naked.
The energy of his wrestling with the things of
time and sense has awakened instincts of which
but for the ardor of that struggle he might
have known little.   He conquers kingdoms, and
weeps like the ancient conqueror.   The world
which he has vanquished cannot satisfy him.
He feels himself to be greater than the universe,
yet feebler than the meanest thing within it
which can follow the appointed law of its being.
The splendor of his material acquisitions is but
a robe too short and thin to wrap him from cold
and shame.   He can *do* great things, but what
is he?   To have all, and to die saying, " *Is this
all?* " is the epitaph of many a rich and wasted
life.   Every fresh region man breaks into reveals new wonders, and with them new enig-
mas, calling upon him to solve them or perish.
There is a social complication, a pressure in our
present day, which is not to be answered by an
unmeaning clamor against rational enlighten-
ment.   We cannot stay the current that is bearing us onwards so swiftly, but we may guide

4 *   F

our course upon it, looking to the stars above.
"Light is good," good for its own sake, whatever it may show us. In an anxious and inquiring age, "when men shall run to and fro, and
knowledge be increased," we are told that "the
wise shall understand." They shall find their
safety, not in placing faith and science in an unreal opposition, not in closing their eyes to the
revelation of God's power, but in opening their
hearts to the secrets of his wisdom "double to
that which is." *

And, now especially that thought and authority are at open issue upon many questions, may
not some among us, ever ready to judge those
who are without, lay to heart the solemn decla-
ration of the Apostle, that judgment must begin
at the house of God! It is so easy to be ortho-
dox in creed and statement; so *safe* to rest in
a merely traditionary belief, that many a deco-
rous Christian fails to perceive the sure though
invisible connection between the lip-confession
and life-denial of a merely outward profession,
and the broader form of denial by which all
such profession is derided. Yet between Christ
mocked and Christ rejected there is but a step;
— who shall say how easily it is taken, or how
quickly we may pass from the hollow homage,

* Job xi. 6.

the "Hail, Master!" which mocks our Lord,
to the smiting and buffeting of open outrage?
When Christ is invested with but the show of
sovereignty, the reed placed in his hands will
be quickly taken, as by the soldiers, to smite
his head. *This reed is nominal Christianity*, a
strange slip of a degenerate vine, beneath whose
blighting shadow a poison-growth of unbelief
never fails to root itself.

And it is certain that this most mournful
characteristic of our age — the disposition to
think slightingly of Christianity,* to ask it what
it has done or can do for the world — has been
helped forward by a want on the part of the
professing Church of whole-hearted faith in its
renewing, transforming energies. Is it strange
that the supernatural revelations of the Gospel
should be looked upon as foolishness by the
world, while they remain — who shall say to
how many among us — a stumbling-block, one
that we dare not remove? but surely there are

* When Jesus was taken before Herod, the king hoped, it is
said, to have seen some great thing done by him, "and he ques-
tioned him in many words, and He answered him nothing." The
attitude of our day is not that of an utter rejection of Christianity.
Like Herod we appreciate and examine into it, questioning it *in
many words* as to what it can do for the world, just as we put the
same question to the schemes of science and philosophy. But to
an age which, like Herod, is deficient in real faith in its Author,
Christianity often answers — nothing. — J. E. B.

systems now in favor, temples made *with hands*, into which we find it hard to fit the stone cut from the rock without hands. Human nature has been ever in love with a modified Christianity, slow to receive Divine truth simply, and as it is given. Hence the dressings and undressings to which Christianity has been subjected. Roman Catholicism has accommodated it to human sense; Rationalism accommodates it to human intelligence, or rather strives to do so; for are those who would make man the measure of all things sure that they have found man's true measure? If the doctrines of Revelation are mysterious, are the facts of Life less so? Are "the things of a man" and the things of God *fitted*, so to speak, by the mere cutting off of all that transcends reason, — itself but a part of man? Reason has its outposts, from which it is continually driven back defeated; it rules, but under a perpetual check; it cannot take account of its own wealth, or fill the region it presides over. It is but a noble vassal, "one that knoweth not what his lord doeth." Man reverences his reason, and trusts it, as far as it will lead him, *but that is not his whole length*, for he feels that he, the reasonable Man, is something greater than it is. Sometimes his dreams are truer than its oracles, and this he

knows.   Therefore one deep calleth to another,
and the answer to this call is Faith.   Faith ad-
dresses itself to man's whole being,—it sounds
every depth; it touches every spring; it calls
back the soul from its weary search within itself,
full of doubt and contradiction; it presents it
with an object, implicit, absolute, greater than
itself,—"One that knoweth all things."   It pro-
vides for every affection, every want and aspira-
tion.   Faith stretches itself over humanity as
the prophet stretched himself above the child, —
eye to eye, mouth to mouth, heart to heart; and
to work a kindred miracle, to bring back life to
the dead, by restoring the One to the One,—*the
whole nature of Man to the whole nature of God.*

Christianity, under its merely perceptive character, has done much for the world ; received as
a law, it has contributed greatly to social order
and well-being; but thus received, it is, like the
Law, too weak to accomplish for any individual
soul the mighty change through which it becomes alive unto God.   For this work is more
than reformative; it asks for a renewing element
— "fire upon earth" — which none save One
coming down from heaven can kindle.   Our
cold, decaying Humanity must be fed by a fuller
life than its own, must be nourished in a warm-
er bosom, before it can attain to any enduring

heat of nobleness or love. If we look through
the long generations that have gone before us,
we shall find that every nobler deed has been
wrought, every fairer life lived, "not after the
law of a carnal commandment, but after the
power of an endless life." The sum of that
great unwritten history lies folded in few
words, — "*All these lived in faith*," in living
faith in a living Person. Shall we look for
those who have done great things for Christ or
for the world among the philosophical admirers
of Christianity, among its formal adherents?

Shall we find them even among those just
persons to whose righteous hearts it is indeed
a law and honorable, but not as yet the law
in which is the spirit of life? Nay, rather
among such as have sought and have received
a Sign, the sign of the Son of Man in heaven,
and in this sign have fought and conquered.
Among superstitious men, believing in many
things, yet believing in Him; among ignorant
men, knowing literally nothing but Jesus Christ
and him crucified, yet knowing him upon no
earthly testimony. Here too lies the quiet, perhaps unspoken secret of those lives of holy, un-
selfish beauty, in which no communion has been
more rich than our own, — to all of these Christ
has come, not by water only, but by blood.*

* Note F.

The foolishness of God, that which **man** counts dark and incomprehensible, is stronger than man, *and nothing else is stronger*. Man loves his own ease, his own labors; there is a sweetness in the natural vine which he will not leave, even at the call to a kingdom, *except for a cause shown*. And hence comes the power of that mighty appeal, the attraction of which He who knew what was in Man prophesied when he said, " I, if I be lifted up, will draw all men unto me." When God, says Bunyan, would tune a soul, He most commonly begins at the lowest note; so has it been in the tuning of the world's wide discord. In the depths of the great atonement God has sounded the lowest note, and to this every life, lived during the last eighteen hundred years in harmony with him, has been attuned. In heaven and upon earth there are

> " Two vast spacious things,
> The which to measure it doth man behoove,
> Yet few there be that sound them, — Sin and Love."

We know little of either until we learn of them at the Cross. There are abysses whose depths can only be guessed at by the weight of the plummet which is required to sound them. Such is sin; it remains, as it has been from the beginning, a dark enigma, drawing thought,

as through some terrible fascination, to fasten
itself on the problem of its existence.*   Here
Reason has transgressed its limits, and Faith
outrun her heavenly guidance.   Wise men, in
their despair of accounting for the origin of
evil, have been driven to deny its existence in
theories too thin to cheat any heart that has
been pierced, yet enlightened, by its sharp reality ; and pious men, falling into the snare which
Job's integrity declined, have " spoken lies for
God, and argued deceitfully for him."   Hence
dreams like that of Optimism,† fictions, such
as evil being but the privation of good ; — names
matter little ; sin desolates as widely, pain racks
as keenly, whether we account for their existence upon a positive or a negative theory.   Yet
it is remarkable that our Saviour, while he does

---

* NOTE BY THE EDITOR. — " And I inquired what iniquity was,
and found it to be no substance, but the perversion of man's will
from Thee, the Supreme, towards lower things." — *St. Augustine.*

" The Scripture, and the Faith, and the Truth say, Sin is
naught else but that the creature turneth away from the un-
changeable Good, and betaketh itself to the changeable, that it
turneth away from the Perfect to that which is in part and im-
perfect, and most often to itself." — *Theologica Germanica.*

" There is no sin but selfishness, and all selfishness is sin." —
Julius Muller.

† It is scarcely necessary to observe that the Christian optimism is as unsatisfactory as the philosophic, and must remain so,
as long as there is no sight so common as that of unsanctified
sorrow and unchastening pain.

not explain this awful problem, *does not explain it away.* To the old, ever-recurring question, " Whence these tares ? " he answers simply, "An enemy hath done this." Man has striven to bridge over this chasm between his soul and God with theories contradictory to the reason they profess to satisfy, and false to the moral sense they desire to soothe; but He who spake as never man spake does not reason upon this subject. He sees this great gulf set; he knows what its mouth has devoured of earth's best and noblest: one thing most precious of all remains ; — he flings Himself within it.

And though this gulf still yawns wide, and stretches itself even unto hell, though it still underlies Nature's fairest scenes, and earth's pomp and beauty and rejoicing descend into it daily, *the beginning of the end has been made.* Sin and pain and death continue their ravages, upheld by him from whom their strength is derived. The Beast lives, yet it has received a deadly wound; its dominion is taken away, though its life is prolonged for a season and a time.

Although the work of renovation is a hidden work, a slow one, " for there are many adversaries " ; though it proceeds as yet among checks and hinderances, as a fair city might rise from its ruins behind a broken and still beleaguered wall, yet the sure foundation has been laid. Deep and wide as decay has struck, the remedy has pierced still deeper. If we must come to the Cross to learn of sin, here too must we come to learn of love, — a love of which we know but little until we see it in its crowning work. For our God is one that hideth himself. Nature, yea also Providence, is thick with dark anomalies; day unto day these utter speech, and night unto night declare knowledge, — a language of sign and parable, *where the voice is not heard;* One is there, only One, who has shown us plainly of the Father. God's bow lies upon the cloud of Circumstance, yet light does not break through it until we see it in the face of Him in whom the excellency of His glory shines. Human life is beset with contradictions, at the solution of which we are but guessers, until Christ solves the riddle that was too hard for us, — bringing forth food and sweetness from the very jaws of the devouring lion. " If thou wouldst have me weep," said one of old, " thou must first weep thyself." *God has wept.* In the strong crying and tears of the Son, in the great drops of sweat as it were blood falling down to the ground, lie the witness to the travail of the

Father's soul. "Herein is love," consoling, rebuking love, — love that has no consolation so strong as the rebuke it administers. "Behold my hands and my feet!" these testify to a necessity endured, an anguish shared. It is our brother's blood that cries unto us from the ground: "A spirit hath not flesh and bones, as ye see me to have."

I often think of George Herbert's homely and affecting verse, —

"Death, thou wast once an uncouth, hideous thing;
. . . . .
But since our Saviour's death
Has put some blood into thy face,
Thou hast grown sure a thing to be desired
And full of grace."

Our Saviour's death has put blood also into the face of life. That which robs death of its sting robs life of its bitterness. When we once realize that the Son of God, in taking humanity upon himself, *took something which he keeps still,* and will not relinquish throughout eternity, we become alive to an awful consolation. We see Creation and its great High-Priest standing as those whom God hath joined together never to be sundered ; and through this living bond, "even his flesh," the anguish of the burden laid upon us, down to the groaning of mere animal existence, arises through a softening medium.　An old Greek litany supplicates Christ by " His known and unknown sufferings."　Who shall say how much the first were exceeded by the last, or fathom the depth of those words, " He tasted death for every man " ? Of the intensity of Christ's sufferings we know and can know little ; *as little, perhaps, of their limits and duration.*　What was the weight of the burden He took upon him in being found as man, and is it altogether laid aside ?　Has He who was once acquainted with grief unlearnt that lesson ?　Has the Man of sorrows, in the persons of his afflicted members, altogether ceased to grieve ?

Was it only for those three and thirty years that the chastisement of our peace was laid upon Him ? only upon the cross that he bore the weight of that which he takes away, — the sins of the whole world ?　The Word on this subject contains utterances into whose depth of meaning only the Spirit can admit us.　I allude to sayings like that of the Master, " Saul, Saul, why persecutest thou me ? " to declarations like that wherein the servant affirms his rejoicing in the sufferings which fill up that which is left behind of the afflictions of Christ.*　These intimations

* How are we to understand the words which tell us of Christ being crucified afresh, and put to open shame by our backslid-

are not dark, neither are they thinly scattered;
they witness to a union more close and intimate
than that through which Christ, *before* his coming in the flesh, redeemed and pitied his people,
and carried them all the days of old. Yet when
we cease to hold to things by the heart, how
little of them do we really retain! We let living facts stiffen into doctrinal abstractions, until

ings? of the Spirit grieved, interceding for us with unutterable
groanings? Are such expressions to be received as merely fig-
urative? Are we, as so many divines have taught us, to believe
that God in using them is but accommodating himself to the
weakness of our human conceptions, and allow ourselves to be
cheated out of the assurance of a Divine sympathy, through the
shallow glosses which have robbed so many Scriptures of their
meaning? God's anger, as inward and outward desolation testify,
is a real thing; so are His love and His pity real, — real as the
nature they spring from, the misery they meet; "and his com-
passions fail not, his mercy endureth forever."

"Veritas est maxima caritas."

The Reformers lay such an almost exclusive stress upon the
work of Christ, that which he does *for* us, that an outside feeling
has crept within the heart of Protestantism; we have light blaz-
ing on us from many windows, but we miss the warmth wh'ch
Catholicism, even Roman Catholicism, has retained, because it
recognizes far more fully than we do the intimate personal communion ever existing between Christ and his body of Elect.
And in this, and not in any idea of meritorious works (a tree
twice dead, plucked up from the very roots), lies the secret of
their extraordinary sacrifices for Him; more particularly as
shown in outward beneficence, and sympathy with the wants
and woes of the human body, — that body of our Humiliation
which He who once condescended to its weakness still bears
upon Him in power.

Truth itself begins to wear a cold and fictitious
aspect: it is not in fact true *for us* until we have
made it our own through needing it, and loving
it. It is not through a merely intellectual recognition that the human spirit can give its Amen
to the yea of God. We see how firm a hold the
Church of the Early and Middle Ages kept upon
this great truth, — the actual presence of Christ
with his people; how this belief revealed, and
as it were transfigured itself in legends which
superstition itself cannot rob of their undying
significance. When St. Francis stoops down to
kiss the leper's wound, and sees that his place
has been taken by the Saviour; when St. Martin hears these words in his vision, " Behold,
Martin, who hath clothed *me* with his cloak,"
we see that the Church to these men is not the
mere tomb of Christ, but his warm and living
body, sending a pulsation through every mem-
ber. There is now among us a disposition to
separate the principles of Christianity from the
facts upon which they are founded. We might
as well attempt to separate the soul from the
body without destroying the Man. For these,
its supernatural facts, are the very life and
breath and blood of Christianity ; *its principles
can only take root in a re-created humanity.*
" Give me a point," said the mechanician, " and

I will remove the world." When Man's soul is effectually moved, it is from a stand-point beyond itself. Experience shows us (as I have said) that Humanity has never been truly built up unto God, but upon the foundation rejected of earthly builders, the mysteries of the Christian faith. Christianity is a building of which as much lies sunk beneath the surface as is reared above it. It is a tree whose roots strike down as deep into the earth as its branches spread wide in the air above, and when we seek to pluck up any one of these roots, a groan goes through its universal frame. We say of earthly things, " that which comes from the heart goes to the heart " ; so it is with heavenly. When Man's heart is touched, it is through that which comes straight from the heart of God. These mysteries, the life and death of God in the flesh, his spiritual resurrection in the reconciled soul of Man, are *messages*, they are God's authentic * love-letters, showing us plainly of the Father.

* Joseph Alleyne, in dying, would often commend the love of Christ, " often speaking of his sufferings and of his glory, *of his love-letters*, as he called the holy history of his life, death, resurrection, ascension, and his second coming, the thoughts of which would ever much delight him."

And to say that the mystery of our Saviour's passion lies at the heart of the whole of man's life in Him is to say little, *for it is that heart itself;* let love or sorrow pierce but a little deeper, and we shall find it even in our own. There is surely something

Those who were first in Christ lived very near the heart of these awful yet tender mysteries. We find them connecting every function of the soul's renewed life with what has been suffered and obtained for it through another life, " of whose fulness we have all received." It is scarcely possible to read the Epistles without feeling that Luther's often-quoted remark, " There is much religion in the possessive pronouns," may be fairly extended to prepositions, so threaded are the whole apostolic writings with these minute, adhesive fibres, — small members of our universal speech, yet boasting great things, as steps in the ladder by which the human spirit ascends even unto heaven.

very affecting in the fact that the sufferings of Christ should lie so much closer to the hearts of his people than all that those sufferings have won for them; that it should be ever the Anguish endured, and not the Glory obtained, which touches all the finest, deepest chords of the renewed nature. I find a proof of this in the fact that dying believers, soon to enter upon

" Zion's habitation,
Zion, David's sure foundation,"

seem to care comparatively little for hymns descriptive of the joys and glories of heaven, beautiful as many of these are. It is to the cross, not to the crown, that the last look turns, the lingering grasp cleaves; and the latest conscious effort of the believer is sometimes to lift himself to Him who was lifted up, through the half instinctive repetition of some words like those of Gerhardt's Hymn on the Passion, the grandest of uninspired compositions:

" O head so full of bruises,
So full of scorn and pain."

By and *through* and *of* and *in* One " *of* whom
are all things, and we *in* him."   It is interesting
to observe that, while the Saints of old appeal
simply to God through his revealed attributes,
his mercy, his faithfulness, his goodness which
endureth forever, it is upon God manifested in
the flesh, in the facts of our Lord's life, and *the
relations which that life has established,* that the
Apostles found their claim.   They rest not so
much upon what God is, as what he has become
to men, their neighbor in Christ Jesus, and as
such bound, as an old divine says, to love them
even as Himself.

> " What hath man done that man may not undo,
> *Since God to man hath grown so near akin?*
> Did his foe slay him? he shall slay his foe;
> Hath he lost all? he all again shall win;
> Is sin his master? he shall master sin."

And if here, as elsewhere, the congregations
of the ungodly have robbed us ; if in the confusion which reigns in the visible churches, it has
become hard for believers to recognize the fact
of their living membership with Christ and with
each other, let us seek more earnestly for the
light* which makes these relations manifest.
We shall not find it in the phosphorescence of
any dead man's candle ; exhalations from the
tombs, though they be the tombs of saint and

* 1 John i. 7.

5   G

martyr, give but an uncertain glimmer. For
it is not galvanic, but organic life we need, and
this is not to be obtained by descending into the
Past to touch the ashes even of a prophet's bones.
They who stand by the grave, even of Christ
himself, may behold, with the devout women, a
Vision of Angels, *but him they see not.* " He is
not here, he is risen. Behold, he goeth before
you into Galilee."

" Man's soul has widened with his world." It
is evident that prescriptive authority must have
now less weight with him than in ruder, less
thoughtful ages. *A child believes things because
he is told them ; a man believes them because they
are true.* To the human spirit is now that word
spoken, — " He is of age ; ask himself."

And it is plain that there was never in this
world's history a time in which, to speak after a
human manner, it was *so easy to miss Christ, so
hard to do without him,* as now. For it is not
only the outward courts that have become wide,
yet crowded ; science continues to open up infinite yet densely peopled spaces, lengthening out,
although every link be golden, the chain between
man's soul and God, so that even the Christian
thinker must respond with sadness to the bold
and satirical saying of Hazlitt, " In the days of
Jacob there was a ladder between heaven and

earth, but now the *heavens have gone farther off*,
and are become astronomical." The very revelation of God's power has tended to weaken the
sense of his immediate presence; yet it is not
here, but in another region, still richer, fairer,
and more perilous, that our peculiar danger lies.
Man, within the limits of his own nature, has
broken into a world of which former ages, and
these the most intellectually subtile and refined,
knew nothing. The time is past when all things
within that nature could be mapped out in broad
and even lines; how many motives and impulses
do we find at work within us of which we cannot say that they are good or evil, only that they
are natural, *human*. Therefore is there a diffi-
culty, ofttimes an agony, introduced into the
Christian life, of which earlier ages were unconscious; partly because the forms of good and
evil were then more definite, and partly because
what Goethe says of the individual holds true for
the race he belongs to; the easy-hearted, even
reckless simplicity of youth, carries it unawares
past many a danger where to pause and to inves-
tigate would be to be lost. For there are voices
that even to hear is bewilderment; shapes that
but to look upon is madness. Our path is beset
with such, alluring, beckoning, inviting us we
know not whither; must we parley, must we

wrestle with each of these to compel it to utter
a clear message, to assume a certain likeness?
The way is long, the day is short; we must onwards, though the leaves above our head mut-
ter, though the flowers that we would pluck are
charactered, though each simple and familiar
thing beside our way has become instinct with
a terrible consciousness, linking it with our own
being. Literature and art, even Nature herself, —
these which for freer spirits had a charm of their
own, and needed not any other, — now breathe
and burn in the fulness of a parasitical life; the
fever of man's conflict has passed across them;
their bloom and fragrance feeds and is fed by
fire kindled far down at the central heart. The
shadow of Humanity falls wide, darkening the
world's playground, and games, be they those of
Hero and Demigod, can no more enthral us.
What is Science itself but a gigantic toy, which
may delight but can never satisfy the heart,
which, even through its sadness and perplexity,
has learnt that it is greater than all that surrounds it? Which confesses that, though the
light within it is too often darkness, still is that
very light " more worthy than the things which
are shown by it "; still are Man's errors greater
than Nature's order, his miseries nobler than her
splendor; still is he

" Chief
Of things God's hand hath fashioned, sorest curst,
Yet holding still the First-Born's birthright, first
In grandeur and in grief."

To know more of ourselves, and to know meanwhile no more of God, makes our present anguish and desolation. But what if even here were our safety? What if it were through this very wound that the good Samaritan as he journeys designs to pour in the wine and oil of his consolation? What if, in learning* more of the awful and tender mystery of our own nature, we become acquainted with the yet more awful, more tender mystery that encompasses it? Never did the heart assert itself so strongly as now; highly strung and sensitive, it finds inward contradiction and outward circumstance bear hard upon it; yet, beset by a thousand warring impulses, it has learnt its own weakness and its own strength, and out of the pressure and straitness of this siege it can take up its appeal to Christ out of the depths and into the depths of a common Nature. It can say, with the blind man, " Jesus, *thou Son of David*, have mercy upon me." It has had its own voice thrown back upon it from the rocks; has seen its own form transfigured upon the mountains; it has had enough of echoes, of illusions; it seeks com-

* Note G.

munion, reciprocity; it needs that which can alone understand, alone *answer* it; therefore the one flies to the one, — the heart to Christ.

And let the heart of man be comforted; it cannot outgrow its Christ; yes, let the heart be comforted in him out of its poverty and its riches alike. When we remember that Christ, in taking unto himself Man's nature, *took upon him all that it would become,* in how glorious and serene a light do the acquisitions of science stand! This thought gives, as it were, music and measure to the onward march of humanity; changes it from an outbreak of tumultuous forces to steady and disciplined progress. And if, turning from the world of action, we flash the light of this truth within the dim and many-chambered region that lies beneath it all, here also we shall discover that in Christ there is a provision, though we may not at once find it, for the growth and expansion which has made Humanity without him like a fruit too heavy for the stalk it hangs on, dragged and trailed to dust by its very weight and splendor. Even through the wealth and apparent waste of ten-drils and suckers it is now putting forth, it may cleave closer, drink deeper unto Him. For all that awakens a sense of need within us draws us by so much nearer Christ; no spiritual truth

being our own until we have needed it ; as long
as we can do without these Divine friends, they
stand in some degree aloof from us, — feeble,
wounded, even despairing, we must cast ourselves upon their very bosoms before they will
receive or return our clasp.

And let us not be discouraged because the
life in Christ has grown less simple than it once
was. In earlier ages, even in times not very
far removed from our own, the Christian's
course was "as straight as a rule could make
it," because the license which surrounded him
compelled him to cast aside all things so as to
secure the one thing alone needful ; to use a
simile of your own, he was like a swimmer casting off his garments, a hard-pressed rider throw-
ing aside his weapons, — to breast the wave, to
win the goal, was all in all.

When the pressure upon faith comes chiefly
from without, this very pressure forces up the
life in a direct, unswerving line like that of the
palm-tree, lifting up its golden abundant crown
to heaven ; the same life would now resemble
that of a banyan, touching earth at many points,
but at every one drawing forth fresh life and
vigor ; less commanding in austere majesty, but
more resembling the tree of prophetic vision,
"a harbor for fowl of every wing." We must

open our minds to this great fact, that all existence is organic; we cannot be, so to speak, one
thing mentally and socially, and another thing
Christianly, as if the life in Christ and the life
in Adam flowed on together yet distinct, like
two unmingling currents. The rational man
will see Christ, as he sees all things, from the
level upon which he, the rational man, stands.
Man cannot see Christ at all except by light
from above; on the hill, as in the valley, we are
in darkness until the dawn breaks; but if sun-
rise finds us upon the mountain-peak, is it not
evident that the prospect its light discloses must
be infinitely wider and more glorious than if it
had overtaken us many degrees lower down?

Now that the whole table-land of existence is
lifted into a higher region, we must discard such
commonplaces as this, that there is no belief like
that of the peasant and the child, and with them
the dark and confused notions of Faith upon
which all such axioms are founded. Faith is
not an extrinsic thing, an outgrowth of the mind
opposed to its rational convictions, its clear and
intimate intuitions. It is reason enlightened by
its Lord and Giver; it is feeling reconciled with
its great object; it is in an emphatic sense " *the
right opinion of that which is.*" As Christ is a
living Person, so is Truth a living thing, that

cannot be nailed like some foreign substance to the mind, but must permeate it, as like draws near to like. Until we see clearly that there is a harmony between that which we receive and that which we are; until we admit that Divine, like human influences, can only do their work upon the soul *through finding a point of contact within it*, we are scarcely so alive to the deep moral significance * of life as to see how it is through that which we believe, approve, yes, even through that which we *like*, that the soul is prepared to receive the impress of Cæsar or of God. "He that is of the truth, heareth my voice." This is a deep saying; so also is that of the prophetic psalm which declares plainly that our Lord reveals himself under aspects varying with the moral and spiritual conditions of those who look upon him : "With the merci-

---

* A significance which runs through it all. Every book, for instance, has a moral expression, though, as in the human face, it may not be easy to say what it consists in. We may take up some exquisite poem or story, with no directly religious bearing, *and feel that it is religious*, because it strikes a chord so deep in human nature that we feel it is only the Divine nature, " God who encompasses us," that can respond to what it calls forth.

From some books, especially such as treat of sin with levity, an odor of death escapes; about others there is an almost sensible savor of life unto life. Some quaint old English poems and devout essays send a fragrance into the very soul; to look into them is to open the tomb of a saint, and find it full of roses.

ful, thou wilt show thyself merciful ; with the
upright man, thou wilt show thyself upright;
with the pure, thou wilt show thyself pure ; and
with the froward, thou wilt show thyself froward."

If spiritual truths were things self-evident,
like mathematical propositions compelling the
assent of the mind they are addressed to, it
would be hard to understand the extraordinary
value which, under the Gospel dispensation, is
attached to Faith. It would be hard to see how
the possession of this one attribute could embalm
as it were a man's whole soul and life ; how a
human being could become dear to his Maker,
simply because he saw that which those around
him were not sufficiently enlightened to perceive.
But is it not evident that this gracious disposition
is one in which the whole man is included ? Is
there not something in the very nature of spiritual Truth which demands for its reception more
than the mere intellect, let it strive as it will,
can compass, and something, too, in our own
nature which makes us, as responsible beings,
answerable for what, as regards this Divine truth,
we see and hear ? To put this in other words,
Can a spiritual truth be apprehended otherwise
than *sacramentally ?* In all cases there will surely
be a proportion between the soul's receptivity

and the fulness that is poured within it; *a measure between what it brings and what it finds.* And
this St. Paul intimates, when he desires for his
Ephesian converts that they may be so rooted
and grounded in love *as to be able* to know that
which passeth knowledge; to enter into that
which he in vain attempts to shadow forth beneath the figures of length and breadth and
height and depth, — the love of Christ, — Love's
secret, which only love itself can make intelligible. " The love of God," saith one of old, "passeth all things for illumination." One drop of
this love shed abroad in our hearts by the Holy
Ghost; one expansion of the renewed mind in
pity, in forgiveness, in love to the Father, in
good-will towards men, will teach us *more of
what God really* is than we could learn from
a thousand disquisitions upon the Divine character and attributes. And that which is the
fulfilling of the law is also, in a great degree,
the understanding of that which it fulfils: for
love has an access, an intuition, of its own; it
attains the end while others are disputing about
the means; it needs not to have every word
explained, defined, interpreted; it is enough for
it *to know the voice*, the voice of the Beloved, to
follow whithersoever that voice leads.

And the voice *of a stranger* the heart will not

follow, even though it be the voice of Christ
himself; therefore would it see more, know
more, have more of Him, faith's sole, sufficing
Object, without whom love in this world would
be too sorrowful, and hope too vague a thing. It
is interesting to observe how the practical spirit
of our day asserts itself in this great demand,
already audible to ears that listen to the under-
swell that rises faint, yet clearly, above the agi-
tating tumult of opinion.   We need the living,
spiritual Christ; and ours are not the needs which
can be satisfied by gazing on his lifeless body,
however curiously embalmed by formalism with
rite and ceremony, neither will we allow mysticism to come by night to steal away his body, and
fill its place with ideas and imaginations of its
own.   For that great demand, " a philosophy of
fruit," has been moved from the kingdom of nature to that of grace ; here too we ask for a vin-
tage, and desire to pass from speculation to that
intimacy with its occupying subject which alone
deserves the name of knowledge.*   Is there not
among us, even amid the very heat and dust of
contending opinion, a manifest weariness of dis-

---

* " There is only one kind of knowledge which can justly be
called wisdom, — *sapientia ;* meaning properly *a knowledge par-
taking properly of the nature of a taste ;* an *intelligere* in which
there is at the same time a *sapere* which appropriates and takes
in its object with a lively relish." — ULLMANN.

cussion? And this from no indifference to dog-
matic truth, *the sure, the only foundation for all
that we can know or can receive of Christ,* but
grounded upon the deep, ever-increasing conviction that even Truth itself, according to Locke's
fine saying, will not profit us so long as she is
but held in the hand, and taken upon trust from
other men's minds, not wooed and won and
wedded by our own.

And here it is that, as regards many questions now at issue, the plain matter-of-fact thinker and the ardent, inquiring Christian find a
common standing-ground. The first will often
ask of those who, whether for scriptural truth or
for apostolic discipline, call upon him to come
and behold their zeal for the Lord, " Where,
among so many notions about the thing, is the
thing itself? Has the fire gone out, or is it still
smouldering beneath the fagots that have been
brought to mend it?" The other, with a deeper
meaning, will inquire, " What is the difference
between placing our confidence in something
which we do, or placing it in something which
we think? We may as well rest in an ordinance
as in an opinion, so long as we rest in either *for
its own sake,* and not for the sake of that which
the confession encloses, the form embodies, —
even the Spirit, which, not to be contained in

these, yet working through them all, converts them into things having life." And thus we have begun to tire of watchwords, to suspect that there is no necessary antagonism between the word which God has spoken and the sign which he has ordained. The Word itself has been made flesh, and has dwelt among us: will objective truth be less valued, Catholic institutions less loved, when each is held dear for the sake of that which it conveys? — even that inward and spiritual grace, the gift obtained by our Lord for us men, the breath, the soul of spiritual life, — a soul which we shall not surely expect to possess more, simply through possessing less of its body. For it is not by rejecting what is formal, but by interpreting it, that we advance in true spirituality; the Spirit of God, even as the spirit of a man, works, and, as far as we yet understand the conditions of our being, *lives*, only through "the body which has been prepared for it." By things which we can see and hear, by things which our hands can handle, by words and forms, by doctrines and institutions, men live, and *in* them is the life of man. For it is neither by that which is merely natural, nor by that which is purely spiritual, that man's complex nature is nourished and sustained: he lives neither by bread alone, nor yet upon angel's food, but upon that in which the properties of each are included, — "the bread which came down from heaven to give life unto the world."

With regard to many of the truths of Christ, we are surely learning to be no more children, ever looking at things "in part," but men, able to appreciate them as they bear upon each other, and upon the facts with which life brings them into relation. And that peculiar condition of our being which makes it hard for us to be altogether "without partiality," which renders it certain that there will be to each believer some one aspect under which his Lord is, above all others dear, some ordinance in which He is above all others present, may, on the whole, help forward the perfect apprehension of Christ. Each individual soul, from the very constitution of our nature, will fasten upon that portion of Divine Truth which meets and answers to its own peculiar need; and when we learn to look at Christianity as a living, organic whole, *made for man, and corresponding with what he is,* we shall the better understand that deep saying of the Apostle's, " There are differences of administrations, but the same Lord "; and understand also how it is that Christianity assumes a distinctive character * in certain ages, among cer-

* Note H.

tain races, even in certain individuals.   Christ
does not so unite himself to Humanity as to
obliterate its native characteristics.   Personality
is a sacred thing, being the very stamp and
print of God upon each human soul: I would
say also, it is an awful thing, being that which,
whatever else we may gain or lose, we keep
through time and through eternity, through it
knowing and *being known.*   And sacred also is
that characteristic impress which, whether in
religious or national society, gives life and individual expression to the community that bears
it.   " Common sense," " public spirit," — are
these mere words?   Words truly, but testifying,
used or misused as they may be, to the fact of
our being, in Adam and in Christ, members one
of another, enjoying not only a separate but a
corporate existence, the functions of which can
only be exerted through fellowship and union.

   " Have we not one Father? hath not one
God created us? and did *He not make* ONE?" *
All civil, as well as all Christian society, is based
upon this confession, yet with this difference,
that the social is the outward, and in some degree conventional, recognition of Brotherhood;
the Christian, its hearty, inward acceptance,
without which the distinctive mark of savage or

* Mal. ii. 10, 15.

animal life will reassert itself in the very bosom
of civilization. Selfishness, or *selfism* (as it
stands in its old form), tends continually to sepa-
ration, — solitariness. Nature, it is true, tells
us that we cannot do without each other, if we
would advance or prosper ; she bids us *use* each
other, Christ bids us *love* each other, " even as
he hath loved us," with no single, no self-cen-
tred aim. He alone setteth the solitary *in families*, by giving, in his own Person, that common
centre for hopes, interests, and affections, which
is the principle of family, — united life. Nature
draws men together, but even in this drawing
there is a disuniting principle at work ; in social
life, for instance, so admirable in its ideal outline, we find practically something in ourselves
and in others which makes it hard, even impossible, to fulfil the obligations that we see most
clearly. We find ourselves in the midst of contending wills, of confused, sometimes contradictory relations, — a strain is laid upon Humanity
which, weak through a civil discord, it is not
strong enough to bear unaided.

"In Adam all dies " ; the flaw runs through
to the foundations, the sword reaches even to
the life. " The earth," saith Christ, " is weak,
and all the inhabiters thereof ; *I* bear up the
pillars of it." Nature and humanity fail ; their

great charter is written in fading characters, dis
tinct, it is true, in outline, but not clearly legi-
ble till held to the warmth of a heaven-kindled
flame. In nature, even as in Christ, no man
liveth, no man dieth, to himself; and of this
human society, even under its most limited conditions, makes us aware, by showing the action
and reaction ever at work between the individual and the community he belongs to. We see
that a man *really* becomes better or worse mor-
ally, advances or retrogrades socially, according
to the standard of life which prevails around
him, — a standard which he himself is at the
same time helping to depress or raise. This is
a truth which we meet by the wayside, and as
often pass without heeding it. Yet once in the
course of this world, in the history of a Man
who lived, who died for the people, who had no
personal interests (as we are accustomed to conceive of them), *and whose life, on any materialis-
tic theory, would have been an impossibility,* this
truth has been taken up upon the Mount, and
there so transfigured and glorified, that men who
toil and struggle below, seeing it in its beauty,
"running to it, salute it." In the life and in
the teaching of Christ, a clear ideal has dawned
upon men, and we must not be discouraged
though we should find it, *like all other ideals,*
hard to be realized in this present life.

The pang of all true spirits in political, in social, in Christian life alike is this, to see clearly what we cannot as yet embrace wholly. Nor must we despair if this pang should grow keener with increasing light;

"As the day lengthens, the cold strengthens."

Two principles are at work within Christianity, twin-existent, of which as yet, travailing and in haste to be delivered, she crieth out, — the desire for unity, and the passionate love for truth. These desires, under the present limitations of human nature, are antagonistic, and have often, in darker ages, torn the bosom at which they were fed. Yet they are no less of Christ, bringing, according to his prophecy, a Sword into the world. We see in the Gentile world no desire for unity, — a desire ever founded on the love, either in earnest or in possession, of some fixed, indisputable truth. And of this they had so little conception, that Pilate's question, " What is truth?" expresses, as it were, the sense of the ancient world. He did not wait for an answer, because he did not believe there was any to be found; all things being true for those who held them to be so. We see how sociable, to use their own expression, the old religions were in this; how ready to adopt and ingraft any new idea or form of belief which seemed good for use, or even for ornament, in social life. We see, too, how opposed to this plastic genius of the Old World is that, the arrow of the Christian Church, which has rankled so sorely in past ages, and even now diffuses a bitterness which, however, if rightly probed, discloses less the bitterness of hatred than that of love, — of love, chilled and mortified, desiring to knit up the ancient bond, yet repelled even while it is attracted, because the iron and the clay are so mixed together that only the heat of charity at its whitest glow can weld them into one. The bosom of Christ is the grave, the only grave of religious acrimony; we learn secrets there which render it possible for us to be of one heart, if we may not yet be of one mind, with all who lean upon it with us. For, slightly as we may think to heal long-festering hurts, there is no cure * for religious dissension except that of spiritual acquaintance with God, as revealed to us in the mind and spirit of Christ Jesus. To "acquaint ourselves" *thus* with God is "to be at peace," for it is to learn how far more strong than all

* Of this the soul's good Physician makes us aware in His memorable answer to his disciples, Luke ix. 54, 55. Even in rebuking their uncharitable temper, he reveals to them its cause and remedy: " Ye know not the Spirit of whom ye are the children."

which separates is that which unites us in Him.
So long as the external is more to us than the
vital, the accidental dearer than the essential, so
long, in short, as we are more Churchmen, more
Protestants, more *anything* than Christians, religious acerbity will continue. It ceases so soon
as the pure language becomes more familiar to
our lips than the dialects in which we are apt to
merge it, and they who are in Christ, *hearing
each other speak plainly*, discover that they are
one in Him, even as he is one with the Father.

"Jerusalem is built as a city that is at unity
with itself"; that which moulds itself from within is free. Who that knows anything of what
unity really is, — how deep its root, how kindly
and unconstrained its expansion, — can be very
solicitous for uniformity, — the outward union of
"*cold and neutral and inwardly divided minds*,"
the rigid, corpse-like symmetry of that which
cannot of itself either live or go, but must be
ever kept up by that by which it can be alone
produced, — the strong pressure of the compelling
hand? Human spirits are only to be drawn together and held together by the living bond of
having found something in *which they really do
agree*. And, though we may yet be far from
the dawning of that day, known unto the Lord,

when Opinion and Truth will be no more at variance, the "One Day* when there shall be One Lord and his Name One," we are, perhaps, not so far removed from a time when devout men, although they be of every nation under heaven, may hear each other speak of the wonderful works of God in their own tongue, — *the tongue in which they were born*, — a speech after which many among us have begun to yearn too fervently to be any longer occupied in framing shibboleths to prove our Brethren.

Is not a day coming — yea, unto them who watch for the Morning, has it not already dawned? — when we shall grow so covetous of good, of grace, as to turn our swords, too often sharpened against each other's bosoms, into ploughshares, to break up the fallow ground that lies within and around us? when we shall beat our spears into pruning-hooks to dress the abundant increase of the days, when the sower shall overtake the reaper, and the treader of grapes him that soweth seed?

Already we are beginning to attach a spiritual meaning to the prophecy, "Ephraim shall not envy Judah, and Judah shall not vex Ephraim"; to look forward to a time when enmity *within* God's kingdom shall so far cease

* See the conclusion of Zechariah's prophecy.

as to allow the kindred zeal of his people, — zeal which is but love under its more ardent aspect, — to be turned against the common enemies of their king, and to find *there* its triumphs. "They shall fly upon the shoulders of the Philistines towards the west; they shall spoil them of the east together; they shall lay their hand upon Edom and Moab, and the children of Ammon shall obey them."

"In the evening time there shall be light." Evening brings with it the thought of home and rest, the desire for communing round the hearth with those of our own family and household. Many steps are now surely,* though perhaps

* "The second Pentecost preceding the coming of our Saviour promises to be of a very universal character. Blessed time! I now read the Old Testament promises of a great blessing 'on *all* flesh' as if I had never read them before: they appear in a new light. Is not that prophecy of Zechariah striking, — 'And the inhabitants of one city shall go to another, saying, Let us go speedily to pray before the Lord, and to seek the Lord of Hosts: *I will go also.* Yea, many people and strong nations shall come to seek the Lord'?

"Those beautiful, questioning words of Isaiah about the Gentiles often occur to me : 'Who are these who fly as doves to their windows ?' — a flock of doves speeding to their home, their ark of refuge. Noah's one dove, like the solitary Jewish Church, took refuge there from the wild waste of waters ; but all kindreds, peoples, tongues, and nations shall fly to their stronghold in latter times, their feathers of gold and their wings covered with silver, white and lovely, though they have lien among the pots." — J. E. B.

half instinctively, seeking the Father's house; there is a sound of home-going feet, a murmur of anxious, loving recognition. The approach of night brings with it a sense of need and dependence, and in this, the World's great evening, the heart has become more alive to the pulsation which is ever at work throughout the whole of Christ's Mystical Body, a secret perhaps not to be entered upon very early in the believer's day. For the characteristic of the religious or seeking soul is solitariness. It is the withdrawal of the soul into the wilderness, there, in that deepened sense of personal accountability in which most religious convictions begin, to plead with God face to face, of individual sin, for individual redemption; its cry is, " Lord, save *me*, for I perish."

The characteristic of the godly, the accepted soul, so joined unto the Lord as to be of one spirit with him, is fellowship; in awaking up into Christ it awakes unto its brethren; its exclamation is that of the Psalmist, " Behold, there are *many* with me."

And though the believer often seems, like his Master, to tread the wine-press alone, neither his conflicts nor his triumphs are ever really solitary. " Multitudes, multitudes," if unseen, are ever round him. Our Lord in his last solemn hour speaks of sanctifying himself *for the sake of* those whom his Father had given him, that they also might be sanctified through the truth ; and though we may be unable as yet to pierce to the heart of all that is included in those words, " *Because I live, ye shall live also,*" * we know enough even now to be aware that heaven and earth are drawn so much the nearer each other for every soul in living communion with Christ. As every waste and barren spot becomes a centre for noisome exhalations to gather in, a haunt for doleful creatures to repair to, so for every piece of territory reclaimed unto God the whole garden of the Lord advances by so much nearer its final blossoming as the rose. And as our seasons grow milder and more healthful because a marsh has been drained or a forest cleared in some remote district, so will the blessing which faith draws down extend far beyond the age or region whence its voice arose. Our warfare with the sins and sorrows of our

---

* Our Lord says, " I am come that ye might have life, and that ye might have it more abundantly "; life in its abundance, not in its mere continuity, which, at least to some spirits, would offer little to attract or satisfy. But what if we receive the saying in its *intensity*, — " the fulness of life," — extended capacities, enlarged affections, with infinite wisdom and love to meet and answer them ? " My people shall be satisfied with my goodness, for I have satiated the weary soul, and replenished every sorrowful soul."

6

spirits may be accomplished in some far-distant field, and they who have tarried at home may thus divide the spoil with the mighty. The lowly Christian, lifting up holy hands to God, is at that moment strengthening those of some unseen brother; the ground upon which he kneels may continue dry as was the fleece of Gideon; the object upon which his heart's desire and prayer is set may fail; yet his labor has not therefore been in vain in the Lord. The blessing he has sought may drop far hence upon the dwellings in the wilderness, may help to bring down floods upon the dry ground which has not of itself craved after the increase from on high.

And knowing that neither the word which God sends forth, nor the holy impulse which that word quickens, can ever return to him void, are we not justified in much hope, in long patience? You say to me, " We ask for the continual dew of God's blessing; but need we, in days when the enemy breaketh in like a flood, despair of seeing floods descend upon a waiting world in answer to secret, persevering prayer?" " I will pour floods upon the dry ground." The ground is dry, yet it still contains within it that Root which sprung of old " out of a dry ground"; a root which at the scent of water will bud and bring forth boughs like a plant. " Revive, O Lord, thy work in the midst of the years ! "

" Awake, O north wind, and come,
thou south ; blow upon my
garden, that the spices
thereof may
flow out."

PART THIRD.

"Therefore, behold, I will allure her,
And bring her into the wilderness,
And speak comfortably to her;

And I will give her her vineyards from thence,
And the valley of Trouble for a door of Hope."

HOSEA ii. 14, 15.

PART III.

"MY soul is athirst for God," saith the Psalmist, "even for the *living* God."

There is a point beyond which neither the experience of others, nor even the utterances of the inspired Word can instruct or comfort the heart; it must have rejoicing in itself, and not in any other; it must learn of its Lord as none save himself can teach. Its prayer is, "*Make me to hear thy voice.*" It knows much about Jesus, *but it desires to know him;* it can no longer rest in opinions, in ordinances, in Christianity received as a system, in anything save in Christ, and in actual communion with him.

But whence comes this sigh, the broken language of every Christian heart, "More of Christ!" How is it that our Lord hath been so long time with us, and yet we have not known him?

Who among us has not experienced moments, and these perhaps often recurring, in which the heart has communed with itself and been sad, desiring that Jesus would himself draw near, yet ready, in its discouragement, to ask whether, in the very urgency of its desire and its endeavor, it may not be exacting too much of itself, may not be expecting too much of God?

For have we, in this urgency, enough considered that saying of our Saviour's, " I have yet many things to say unto you, *but ye cannot bear them now* "?   The natural man dies hard within us; the man from heaven is not born* without a pang; first the Anguish, then the Joy.   Are our souls willing, yea, are they *able*, to endure that anguish, ardently as we may desire the joy which makes it to be remembered no more? When the fulness of time is come, the fulness of strength will be given to meet it, and not before; and, meanwhile, the way of life continues to have its own ache,† a sadness peculiar to itself.

A certain degree of impatience seems natural, even befitting to Man, a being of keen though limited vision, of stringent though narrow grasp.

---

* " *We know not,*" says Bacon, speaking of natural life, " *whether to be born may not be as painful as to die.*"

† Kein Reisen ist ohn Ungemach,
  Das Lebensweg hat auch sein Ach.

His mind, as one who has sounded its very
depths has taught us, is naturally enamored of
order and system; he finds within himself the
Surmise of a perfection which outward nature
does not respond to, and for this he the more
delights to trace a sequence through all her apparent confusion; to discover that by earth and
air and ocean there is *a path* such as the vul-
ture's eye hath not known. And if science, as
has been truly said, mourns to find a gap, every
here and there, in her great chain of cause and
consequence, — a link broken, perhaps dropt
through forever, — how is it with the Christian,
if in the ladder which joins earth to heaven
there should be some rounds wanting? How
is it when Man, who loves to track the end from
the beginning, to see the flower wrapt up in the
bud, finds that the life of the soul, like that of
the insect, must pass through strange metamor-
phoses, through sundry successive kinds of
deaths? when he discovers that the life of the
Divine seed, set so deep in the heart and in the
world, instead of being one of consistent growth,
of free, harmonious development, may be the
most fitly illustrated by the well-known simile
of an acorn set within a jar of porcelain; a
mighty plant that must shatter its frail earthen
tabernacle in its growing.

6 *   I

And here we are reminded of what the prophet tells us, that God's thoughts are not our thoughts, neither His ways our ways. God has time for everything, and he has room for everything; but it is far otherwise with his creature, and the tendency of all human effort is to go straight to a desired aim, putting on all possible strain and pressure. Thus, adding what we conceive of infinite power *to what we know of finite will*, we have arrived at an idea of Omnipotence,* the exact opposite, surely, of that to

---

* An idea in which we lose sight of the fact that God, no less than man, has a nature, and within that nature laws by which he is irresistibly governed, and ends to which his designs infallibly tend ; and it is probable, indeed certain, that, if we could see clearly into the depths of the Divine counsels, we should find nothing arbitrary or adventitious in any of the works or decrees of the Almighty ; nothing, I mean, which *could have been otherwise than that which it is.* Choice is the glory of humanity, its distinctive attribute ; raising a man as high above the inferior creatures as it sinks him below Deity, for to choose is obviously as human as is to err ; infinite wisdom can see and take but one way.

God, as his Apostle tells us, *cannot* deny or contradict himself; and upon this, His moral obligation, the moral freedom of man is founded, — a freedom which the gospel of life and immortality has brought to light, and which it alone reveals. All systems founded upon nature gender to bondage ; behind which of these, whether Pagan or Pantheistic, do we not see, or rather feel, the dark background of *power only*, — in other words, Fate, decreeing, creating, devouring all things, — the blind, impassive womb and grave of rational and sensitive life ?

"God is a spirit." What is Predestination, the Christian form of Fatalism, but this, — the everlasting purpose of God *towards*

which all *we see* of the Almighty's works would lead. We accustom ourselves to speak of his dealings, whether in grace or nature, as being sudden, irresistible, one in design and in execu-

good, which sin by its very nature contradicts, and naturally opposes, so that that which is exceeding good becomes the exceeding evil ("anguish, tribulation, and wrath") of those who resist it. The ungodly, unless, through repentance and faith in Christ, they fall back, as it were, upon God's plan, *must* perish with all that runs counter to it. Consider in this light the maledictory passages in the Psalms, and the awful denunciations of the Prophets against national sins; they are declaratory, having to do with what *is,* as much as with what will be. The spirit instructed in God's unchanging counsels (knowing His mind and purpose) reads the Present and Future by one light, and is able to interpret the one by the other. What *has* been (in this sense) *will* be, *must* be; under certain conditions certain results follow.

NOTE BY THE EDITOR. — The awful question here touched upon has been too often presented by theologians in such a way as to shock the moral sense, by a necessary inference that the Divine economy is alike conservative of evil and good, misery and happiness. Implacable hate, immeasurable revenge, insatiable cruelty, — all that is abhorrent in man, — have been attributed by the veriest blasphemy of logic to God. Eternity of evil, an endless, aimless horror of discord, torment, and despair, believed in as an end and purpose of creation, would seem to make heaven itself impossible. Our author, while admitting the fact of future suffering and loss, refers it to that conscious freedom of choice inseparable from man as a moral being, the denial of which in this life or the next involves the loss of his personal identity and accountability. The dark problem has no other solution than that which is reached through simple faith in the Divine Goodness. Shall not He do right? Can we not leave all in His hands? If we, when nearest to Him in feeling, yearn with tenderest pity after the sin-sick and suffering, how much more He whose name is Love? Overwhelmed by a sense of our own moral infirmities

tion ; yet Nature, so soon as ever we pierce below her broad surface-smile, betrays on every hand the marks of care, of patience, and adaptation. All that we learn of God in this region tends

and the evil about us, we are too prone to question the sufficiency of His love; bound down, as it were, in the grave-clothes of spiritual death, we too often distrust " the power of His resur rection." " Infinite Goodness," says the Countess de Gasparin, " finds us more sceptical than infinite justice." Sin indeed throws a baleful shadow upon the future; but who shall set limits of time and place to the mercy of God, which "endureth *forever*"? " When," asks the author of this book in her closing paragraph, " were Love's arms stretched so wide as upon the cross?" Looking thitherward, may we not tremblingly and reverently trust the larger hope, which, secretly cherished in the inmost heart of Christendom from the times of Origen and Duns Scotus to those of Foster and Maurice, has found its fitting utterance in the noblest poem of the age?

> " O yet we trust that somehow good
>   Will be the final goal of ill,
>   To pangs of nature, sins of will,
> Defects of doubt and taints of blood:
>
> " That nothing walks with aimless feet,
>   That not one life shall be destroyed
>   Or cast as rubbish to the void
> When God hath made the pile complete:
>
> " That not a worm is cloven in vain;
>   That not a moth with vain desire
>   Is shrivelled in a fruitless fire,
> Or but subserves another's gain.
>
> " Behold! we know not anything:
>   I can but trust that good shall fall
>   At last, — far off, — at last, to all,
> And every winter change to spring."

more and more to bring his works out of the
domain of the *magical*, to convince us that it is
the human, and not the Divine energy, which
craves for its purposes the signet-stamp of full
and speedy accomplishment ;

> " For we are hasty builders, incomplete;
> Our Master follows after, far more slow
> And far more sure than we, for frost, and heat,
> And winds that breathe, and waters in their flow,
> Work with Him silently."

And turning to God's inner kingdom ; here,
too, where the good to be desired is so great,
the evil to be avoided so imminent, even here,
also, we must confess that God wraps up his
great designs in a husk or envelope, which will
not fall from off them until the appointed time
be come. What is the sacred history, from its
very beginning, but that of a labor working to
a mighty, far-seen, and remote end ? What is
Christianity, though it has in its cradle contend-
ed with and crushed the serpent ? — even now
but "an infant of days." We think, naturally,
that God might make all things as he wishes
them to be at once ; but we find that it is not
his way to do so. God does not heal us with
a touch. He uses means and processes, tedious
often and peculiarly afflicting, — " He giveth
medicine " for our mortal sickness ; *a life-long*

remedy for a life-long ill. And when we feel —
as what Christian at times does not ? — an impatience with the slowness of our own growth,
let us look from ourselves into the universal
Church of Christ, and ask this self-answering
question of our hearts, *How shall the growth of
the part be rapid, when that of the whole has been
so slow?* Let us consider the nature of the
Earlier Dispensation, and recollect under how
many costly and cumbrous folds of rite and
ceremony the treasure of the world lay hid.
Let us remember that this is *still* a hid treasure; that to the outwardly Christian, no less
than to the Heathen World, the great mystery
of redeeming love remains that world's Open
Secret, *declared, yet uncommunicated,* plain to
the ear, yet dark to the sense. Let us consider the slow, the uneven, the painful advance
of the Mystic Spouse, — she that cometh up
from the wilderness, leaning upon the arm of
Her Beloved, — and we shall see that she, like
her Lord, is wounded in her heart, her hands,
and her feet.

And that these things are so, the Christian
must fain confess. Yet he would fain see them
otherwise; would fain behold if it were but
the initial fulfilment of those deep, instinctive
prophecies which overcharge his heart, — *a*

*heart too large for the body through which it must
for the present work.* Yet, among many yet
unfulfilled predictions, he must look upon one
evermore fulfilling itself, and read in all that
passes within him and around him a comment
upon the Eldest-born of Prophecy: " Thou
shalt bruise his head, *and he shall bruise thy
heel.*" He must see evil following hard upon
good, *following because of good;* Satan exalting
himself against Christ; the Gates of Hell ad-
vancing upon that against which they shall
never prevail. Therefore is he often in this life
perplexed and baffled, as one that knoweth not
what his Lord doeth. And it is this which
gives such terrible, even blighting power to the
words and writings of unbelievers, which barbs
and sends home many a dull scoff that would
otherwise fall harmless, — that they touch a conscious, ever-rankling wound. *What they urge
against Christianity is true.* The believer
knows, already knows, all that the infidel can
tell him ; the eye of love can see as clearly as
that of hate, and it has already mourned over
all that the other exults in ; has seen springs
sink down suddenly among the sands of the
desert ; has looked upon bare and stony channels, now ghastly with the wreck and drift of
ages, yet showing where once a full, fair river

bore down life and gladness to the ocean.   The Christian would fain explain, account for, these long delays, this partial efficacy, this intermittent working.   He feels that he is in possession of the key which is to open all these intricacies, but at present he finds that, like that of the Pilgrims, " it grinds hard in the lock."   He sees Jesus, but he sees not yet all things put under him.   The world around him is the same world which crucified his beloved Lord, and he must listen from age to age to its insulting cry, " If thou be the Christ, come down from the Cross, and we will believe."

There is something sorrowful, even perplexing, in every life which is guided by a standard which those around us do not recognize ; to be living by the dial, when all around us go by the clock, brings a contradiction into the life of which the lives of those who are in league with circumstance, " the slaves and the masters of every day," know nothing.

There is a sadness in all Idealism ; it lifts the soul into a region where it cannot now dwell ; it must return to earth, and it is hard for it not to do so at the shock of a keen revulsion, the dashing of the foot against a stone.   But in no life does the secret of all tragedy,* the conflict

---

* Interior freedom and exterior necessity, these are the two poles of the Tragic World. — F. Schlegel.

between the Will and Circumstance, so unfold
itself as in that of the Christian ; he, of all men,
feels and mourns over that sharp, ever-recurring contrast of our existence, — the glorious
capabilities, the limited attainments, of man's
nature and destiny below. For *his* possibilities
are at once more glorious and more assured
than those of other men ; yet, as regards actu-
alities, he among all men must be content to
have the least to show. And this, if we examine deeply, will be found at the root of all
sincere fanaticism. It is the agony of the spirit,
its strict, convulsive embrace of some glorious
truth, the soul's first love,* for the sake of which
it refuses to perceive the limitations to which all
things here have been made subject. Having
tasted of the fruit of the tree of life, " good for
food, pleasant to the eyes, and to be desired to
make one wise," it forgets that old, unrepealed
statute, that man, in the Second Adam as in the
First, must till the ground from whence he was
taken.† Until he returns to the earth, he must
turn to it, nourishing and being nourished by it;
if he would stretch forth his hand and live by
what he can reach of absolute truth, he will
quickly come across the flaming sword turning
every way to keep the way of the Tree of Life.

    * Note I.   † Genesis iii. 19, 23.

"We trusted it had been He which should have redeemed Israel." Under whatever form this hope encounters us, — from the wild excesses of the Fifth-Monarchy Men and Munster Anabaptists, to the simple expectation of the Dorsetshire peasant, who in Monmouth's rebellion talked about " King Jesus," — there is always something affecting in its expression ; and the more so, because the foreseen sadness of its disappointment is one which connects itself with the natural experience of Christian life. How much is there in this to remind the believer of what the two chosen disciples must have felt when they descended from the Mount of Transfiguration! For he, too, has known moments, perhaps hours, on which the calm of eternity seemed already to rest, — still, blessed seasons in which he has beheld, not only Moses and Elias, but his own life also, transfigured in his beloved Lord ; *times in which things present were intelligible, things distant clear.* And he, too, has come down, like them, to meet the full shock of this life's perplexity, to be met by human anguish, the struggles of the demoniac, the tears of his father, to witness and perhaps share the discomfiture of his brethren, " Why could not *we* cast him out ? " to listen to their perverse disputings as to " who among them should be greatest."

To whom shall he declare the glorious revelation? to whom shall he even speak * of the things which he has seen and heard? Yea, even while he thinks upon the Vision, even before it has had time to fade, he may find, by a sudden blank and stillness in his own spirit, that " it has been received up again into heaven."

"A little while!" said the disciples; "what is this he saith? A little while! — we cannot understand what he saith." *A little while, and ye shall not see me,* — a hard saying to the loving, confiding heart, which would fain abide forever where it has found it so good to be, — a hard but

---

* " *All that I hold worthiest,*" says David Scott, of the high ideal objects to which his life was devoted, " *seems to remove me from the sphere of other men.*" A kindred sense of isolation must often overtake the Christian, and it is one which he must learn to meet with a prepared and patient heart. We must be content faithfully to speak out what we feel and know, without expecting that others will be proportionably affected. These things have been *shown* to us by God himself, worked by His Hand into the very frame and texture of the soul; can the mere *telling*, even though of truth itself, affect as sensibly?

Besides this, we must remember that it is not only spiritual things that appear "foolishness" in the absence of enlightened receptivity. Young people, for instance, do not, *cannot*, believe what the old tell them of life and its trials; and what mere jargon, to one uninitiated, appears the talk of two enthusiasts upon literature and art! It gives him a secret irritation; he is not only uninfluenced by their zeal, but scarcely believes that they themselves really feel what they express so strongly, knowing that the world to him goes on very well without this foreign element, and could dispense with it forever.

inevitable saying. There is a severity in our Lord's inner discipline which reminds the believer of Joseph's making himself strange unto his brethren. For it is not the natural man only that has to be humbled and chastened by Him, the spiritual man also must become as a weaned child, and for him there is "a secret, low fire" kept long burning. In Christ, as well as for Christ, they are to be counted happy who endure; who bear all things, — silence, delay, aridity, for thus he trains his Athletes.

The spiritual life is a world within itself; with joys, with sorrows, I would say also with *temptations*, peculiarly its own; and he has not advanced far within its borders who has not learnt the truth of that saying, " I beheld, and, lo! by the very gate of heaven was there a road to hell," who has not prayed with holy Herbert for deliverance "*from the arrow that flieth by noonday.*" There is much even in the renewed mind which, if suffered to remain there, would gradually eat away the heart of its strength and purity; something in each believer, which he imagined he had left behind when he forsook all and gave himself up to follow Christ, but he finds that it has rushed after him, like Care in the ancient proverb, and holds to him with as tight a grasp as ever.

How many tendencies, and these not to be numbered among such as are the least worthy, will seek, like Clovis and his Paladins, for a hollow, hasty baptism, that they may be called by Christ's name, and fight his battles, remaining just what they were at first! Therefore the believer, as he advances in self-knowledge, learns to bless and to adore those piercing yet enlightening experiences of his own weakness, which, as it were, let daylight within his whole spiritual being. He learns, even in exclaiming, " Who shall deliver me from the body of this death ? " to rejoice in those its deep-seated infirmities, against which he continually prays and strives, — he finds many things within him, pitiable rather than sinful ; hinderances from which he longs to free himself, yet learns even in these to recognize his true though humble friends and helpers ; *him they compel to bear the cross ;* and even in that compulsory bearing, his heart so grows to it, as to desire no independent strength or virtue. " *Blessed are ye poor.*" Blessed are the souls in whom not the strength of nature only, but that of grace, has been so brought low, even to the very dust, that they have learnt to call nothing that they have their own.

Often must the believer, like Antæus, grow stronger for having touched the ground ; often must he experience the sentence of death *in himself*, — must feel himself a Being without heart or hope, incapable and even insensible, so that he may learn to trust, not in himself or in any other, but in Him who raises the spiritually dead.   The Christian must hold on to God, through conflicts and agonies; he must fight while his blood runs down and glues his hand to his sword, so must he hold on, when that hand* is benumbed and stiff with cold; when strength and consciousness seem gone together, and only an instinct remains through which the soul is able to fling itself like a dead weight upon Christ.   Yet even here is

* The fluctuations to which spiritual life is subject show the wisdom and goodness of God in making so much of it to reside in duty, *a principle independent of the variations of feeling.* There are long seasons of banishment from God's presence, unconnected, perhaps, with any sense of His displeasure, in which the soul must say, " Make me as one of thy hired servants," and during which, even in the absence of sensible love and joy and fervor, it may be able to testify that " *Great is the peace of them that love thy law.*"

There are spaces and silences in the Christian life, times which it is impossible to describe, because " full desertness " in souls, as in countries, " lieth bare," — times when the soul seems devoid of the capacity, even of the desire, for communion with its Lord, yet even during these its delight in His service may continue, because the excellency of His commandment has truly, however imperfectly, become its chief and chosen good. " *The poor,*" saith our Master, " *ye have ever with you,* but *Me ye have not always.*" A continual service of love, but a communion not as yet abiding.

" An overthrow
Worth many victories."

Through being chilled and mortified in the small-
est, most inwardly humiliating things; through
being beaten away from the broken cisterns of
self and of all creatures, we learn, as we could
never without this have done, to look to Christ
as our well of life, and so to find *all* our fresh
springs in him, as to be able to say with a simple
and sincere heart, " Lord, give me evermore of
this water, so that I thirst not, neither come
hither to draw."

" He that believeth shall not make haste."
Blessed are they, thou good Joseph, who love
thee even as thou art; who trust thee in spite
of thy silence and thy strangeness, thy long delays, thy repeated questionings, thy withdrawal
into thy secret chamber, thy protracted tarrying
there. " Blessed is he who shall not be offended
in Me."

For Wisdom, even in this world, is justified
of her children; most so of all in Him, her chief,
her only beloved Son, without Whom was not
anything made that was made, yet who rejoices
in the *habitable* parts of the earth, and whose
delights are with the sons of men. I know not
how to speak of that great era in the Christian's
soul when, whether through the Strength of a

patient following, or through the sweetness of a loving recognition, it *finds* Him whom it has long loved, and passes,* in that finding, from the straitened life within itself into the free outlooking from self into Christ. When it ceases to confer with flesh and blood, to watch over its own changes and fluctuations, for the sake of attaching itself implicitly to Him who is the whole of what we have in part; when it lives no longer by faith,† but by Christ, holding Him

---

* "I have loved thee with an everlasting love, therefore with loving-kindness have I drawn thee." After long conscientious serving of God, refreshed by little feeling of joy or comfort, there are moments when the soul seems suddenly made aware of its own happiness, — when, either through outward circumstances or without them, an appeal is borne in upon it as direct, as pleading, as distinct, as that which was made of old to Peter, "Simon, son of Jonas, lovest thou me?" and it is able to answer out of its very depths, "Lord, thou knowest." Its love for its Lord being as surely felt, as little to be doubted as its own being, it answers as steadfastly as if asked whether a parent or child was loved — it dares even to appeal to the omniscience of the heart-searching God, — "*Thou knowest.*" Such moments are surely more to us than a passing comfort. Do they not teach us something of the depth of those words, "*We love him because he first loved us.* For is not this also of the Lord, — this tender attraction, this warmth, at which the frozen waters of the heart break up and flow forth as at the breath of spring? And does not this seeking of our love on Christ's part convince us that he is ever loving us in our colder as well as more fervent seasons, and that, in being drawn by his loving-kindness, we have laid hold on his everlasting love, — a chain which runs backwards and forwards through all eternity? — J. E. B.

† Note K.

too surely to think of that it holds by, — it
has done with self-questioning, with self-analy-
sis; *it believes in the love by which it lives*, and
can appeal for all answer to the fact of its own
life.

And I know not what should more cheer and
gladden a Christian than to see his spiritual life
losing everything of an exotic character; to have
it set in the open air, welcoming the wind from
every quarter; acquiescing in all things *because
depending only upon one.* A free and sustained
spirit becomes habitual to him, who, in the breaking of his daily bread, has found that Real Presence which sanctifies and glorifies our life's poor
Elements. When the heart has found its true
gravitation, it leaves that Rest slowly and returns to it quickly; disturbing influences will
be felt from time to time, but their power is
gone, — "*that which is the strongest must win.*"
A firm, assured patience grows upon the Christian, enabling him to hold upon his way, unde-
terred, unchilled, by whatever he may meet
upon it; enabling him also, I know not to
what inner music, to build up his spirit to a
Strength of calm, reliant conviction, even with
the stones he finds there, as a brook lifts up
a more clear and rapid voice for flowing over
pebbles. Roughness and littleness, indifference

7   J

and contradiction, for all of these the heart that has made room for Christ finds room, in a steadfast, not scornful allowance.

The strain upon the inner life has passed over from self to Christ, and with that strain the uneasy pressure which may once have tended to something of exaggeration and eccentricity. Time was when the believer was often fain, with the Gaul of old, to decide a doubtful question by violence, to fling his sword within the wavering balance. He can now afford, like the practised archer in sending home his arrow, to allow for the set of the wind it flies through. His heart has grown wise, instructed, tolerant, tender with weakness, patient of imperfection:

> " Who is blind as he that is perfect,
> And blind as the Lord's servant? "

How quiet such a life is! how fruitful!—fruitful because it is so quiet; it works not, but lives and grows. The uneasy effort has passed out of it; *unresting, because it rests always,* it has done with task-work and anxiety; it serves, yet is not cumbered with much serving; it has ceased from that sad complaint,—" *Thou* hast left me to serve *alone.*"

Such a life will seem less spiritual only because it has grown more natural; the soul moves in an atmosphere which of itself brings it into

contact with all great and enduring things, and
it has only to draw in its breath to be filled and
satisfied. I know not how to describe the grandeur and simplicity of the state that is no longer
self-bounded, self-referring; how great a thing
to such a freed and rejoicing spirit the life in
Christ Jesus seems; a temple truly "not of this
building," too great to be mapped out and meas-
ured;* *too great to be perfect here.* A thought
for which our mortal life, — a language as yet
too broken and confused to

" Catch up the whole of love and utter it," —

can find no corresponding word.†

Yet Experience, even the deep assurance
of our present imperfectibility, worketh Hope.
Though the Church, like the moon, seldom
reflects the clear outline, never the full splendor
of the light she shines by; though the shadow

---

* Note L.

† De Quincey, speaking of the grandeur and subtility of the
human spirit, says most beautifully, that all of our thoughts have
not words corresponding to them; many of them in our yet imperfectly developed nature can never express themselves in acts,
but must lie, *appreciable by God only*, like the silent melodies in a
great Musician's heart, never to roll forth from harp or organ.

In connection with this idea, in how sublime a light does His
Name — THE WORD — place our Saviour. Jesus Christ is the
Word of God, him in Whom the Father's thought has found full
and perfect utterance. " For I know the thoughts that I think
concerning you," saith the Lord, " thoughts of peace, and not of
evil, *to give you an expected end.*"

of earth is too often cast between her orb and
Him, she is still "the faithful witness in
heaven," weakness girt about with power, the
Woman clothed with the Sun, a Wonder in
earth and in heaven.   Though the believer is
no plant grown up in his youth, fair and
flourishing, without blight or mildew; though
he may be far indeed from sealing up the sum,
"full of wisdom and perfect in beauty," still,
in spite of every warp and hinderance, *he has
grown*, and his life has become to him but a
Prophecy of the life it keeps warm within it, —

> "Close comprest,
> Our Present holds our Future, like a Rose
> That may not yet its perfect Soul unclose,
> Lest angry winds should scatter or molest."

And as the Christian advances upon his way,
a sweet and solemn sense of the unity of life
grows upon his spirit. "We are complete in
Him"; much of our life, if viewed in itself
only, would appear purposeless and broken, yet
Christ has said, "Gather up these fragments
that remain, so that nothing be lost." We
learn to look at life as a whole thing; not to be
discouraged by this or that adverse circumstance, remembering how much there is and
will be in that life which is "like frost and
snow, *kindly to the root*, though hurtful to the

flower," fatal to the bloom and fragrance, the lovely and enjoyable part of our nature, but friendly to its true, imperishable life. Looking at ourselves, we may see that, under a slight, sometimes a very slight, modification of inward bent, or outward circumstance, we should have been far more happy, more beloved, *apparently* more useful than now ; yet we may also see as plainly, as we confess it humbly, that we have attained, through all these losses, to that to which every gain is even present, appreciable loss. And here I would gladly say something of those gracious outward providences through which God will sometimes *visibly* visit and refresh the spirit, turning over, perhaps forever, a tear-stained page of contradiction, and unfolding a fresh leaf of richer, happier experience ;

"For not forever will he continue thus to thresh it,
  Not to vex it with the wheel of his wain,
  Nor to bruise it with the hoofs of his cattle.
        .   .   .   .   .
  In just measure when thou inflictest the stroke, thou wilt
      debate with her,
  With due deliberation even in the rough tempest."

Gradually, almost imperceptibly, the believer will find the current of his existence sweeping into a broader channel ; will find " doors opening " upon him, doors of happiness, doors of

usefulness, which will be to him a Gate of
Heaven; "windows opening," letting in the
breath of summer upon his soul, filling it with
sunshine and sweet air; suddenly too, in the
deep emergencies of life, some new interest,
some friend, will appear like the Great Twin
Brethren, or Saint of old, in the thick of the
battle, vanishing perhaps when the fight is over,
yet blessing him even in vanishing from his
sight.

For that terrible saying of Anne of Austria
to Richelieu holds true for mercy as well as for
judgment: " My Lord Cardinal, God does not
pay at the end of every week, but at the last *he
pays*." God may put his faithful ones upon a
long and painful apprenticeship, during which
they learn much and receive little, — food only,
and "that in a measure," — often the bread
and water of affliction. Yet at the last *he
pays ;* pays them into their hearts, pays them
into their hands also. We may remember long
seasons of faint yet honest endeavor; the pray-
ers of a soul yet without strength; the sacrifices
of an imperfectly subdued will, bound even with
cords to the altar; we may remember such
times, or we may forget them, but their result
is with us. Some of the good seed sown in
tears is now shedding a heavenly fragrance

within our lives, and some of it will blossom, perhaps bear fruit, over our graves.*

There are moments in the Christian life upon which the spoil of a long conflict seems heaped, in which it can rejoice even with the joy of a late yet abounding harvest. Seasons, too, sometimes prolonged ones, which recall what the historians of the Middle Ages tell us of the Truce of God, — set, appointed times when the land had rest, and war and violence were no more heard within its borders; so are there blessed intervals, wherein the soul reckons up many desolated Sabbaths, and enjoys a God-given, God-protected rest.

Light is good, and it is a pleasant thing to behold the sun. Yet far dearer than outward peace, far sweeter than inward consolation, is that, the ever-during stay, the solace of the Christian's heart, the imperishable Root of which all else that gladdens it is but the bloom and

---

* "I have remarked," says Palissy, "trees and plants which felt their decay approaching, and which before death hastened to bring forth fruit and grain before the accustomed time. — What if I spoke of men?"

We may compare what our Saviour says, "Except a corn of wheat die, it abideth alone, but if it die, it bringeth forth much fruit," with the fact that his brethren, who did not believe on him during his life, were, after his death, in two known and other probable cases, his devoted followers and martyrs.

odor; the dry tree* that shall flourish when
every green tree of delight and of desire fails.
It is to the Cross that the heart must turn for
that which will reconcile it to all conflicts, all
privations; which will even enable it, *foreseeing
them*, to exclaim, "Yet more." When Christ
is lifted up within the believing soul, nothing is
too hard for it to venture upon or endure; it
rests upon a power beyond itself, and can bring
its whole strength to bear upon generous, exalted enterprise. Show thy servant *thy work*,
and his own will be indeed easy! Let this
powerful attraction be once felt, the heart's, the
world's great and final Overcoming, and all
other bonds will weaken, all other spells decay.
"*Midnight is past*," sings the sailor on the
Southern Ocean, — "*Midnight is past; the Cross
begins to bend.*"

Outward duties weary, inward consolations
fail. *Charity never faileth.* Let us now turn aside
and look upon this great sight, — of Love that
burneth with fire, yet is not consumed; of Love
that, having poured out its soul unto death, yet
liveth to see of that soul's long travail and to be
satisfied with it. "Behold the Lamb of God,
that taketh away the sins of the world." When
were Love's arms stretched so wide as upon the

* Ezek. xvii. 24.

Cross? When did they embrace so much as
when thou, O Christ, didst gather within thy
bosom the spears and arrows of the mighty to
open us a Lane for Freedom!

" Thou art gone up on high; thou hast led
captivity captive: *thou hast received
gifts for men ;* yea, for the
rebellious also, that the
Lord God might
dwell among
them."

Notes.

NOTES.

NOTE A. — Page 51.

O LORD, what a wonderful spirit was that which made St. Paul, in setting forth of himself against the vanity of Satan's false apostles, hand in his claim here that he in Christ's cause did excel and surpass them all? What wonderful spirit was that, I say, that made him to reckon up all his troubles and labors, his beatings, his whippings, his scourgings, his shipwrecks, his dangers and perils by water and by land, famine, hunger, nakedness and cold, with many more, and the daily care of all the congregations of Christ, among whom every man's pain did pierce his heart, and every man's grief was grievous unto him? *O Lord, is this Paul's primacy, whereof he thought so much good that he did excel all others?* Is not this Paul's saying unto Timothy, his own scholar, and doth it not pertain to whosoever will be Christ's true soldiers? Bear thou, saith he, affliction like a true soldier of Jesus Christ. This is true; if we die with Christ, we shall live with him; if we suffer with him, we shall reign with him; if we deny him, he shall deny us; if we be faithless, he remaineth faithful: he cannot deny himself. This Paul would have known to everybody; *for there is no other way to heaven but Christ and his way.*" — Bishop Ridley's *Farewell Letter to his Fellow-Prisoners, and those who were exiled for the Gospel of Christ.*

——◆——

Note B. — Page 54.

"KNOW you what our Saviour says to his dear Peter? ' *When thou wast young, thou didst gird thyself, and didst walk where thou wouldst: but when thou shalt be old, thou shalt stretch forth thy hand, and another shall gird thee, and lead thee whither thou wouldst not.*' (St. John xxi. 18.)

"The young scholars in the love of God gird themselves; they choose their penance, resignation, devotion; they do their own will in doing the will of God. But the old masters in that love suffer themselves to be bound and girded by another; they go by ways which they would not choose according to their own inclinations; they stretch forth their hands, allowing themselves to be governed willingly against their will; they say that '*obedience is better than sacrifices*'; they glorify God, crucifying not only their flesh but their spirit." — *St. Francis de Sales.*

Note C. — Page 57.

IN one of Vinet's works on the Christian life are some excellent remarks on St. Paul's words, "the feeble members are the more necessary." Their silent, unseen work, so humble in its mode of action that sometimes its value is first learnt through the sensible blank its withdrawal leaves, is lasting work because it is real work, done and followed, if followed at all, "for the work's sake." But it is evidently far otherwise when genius, learning, or extraordinary force of character, *things which have a powerful attraction in themselves*, are consecrated to the service of Christ. In spirits thus gifted — its burning and shining lights — the Church must be willing to rejoice "for a season," for much that they bring with them will depart when they go; the foreign elements will break up and scatter when the cord which binds them together is slackened by absence or unloosed by death. We see this in the lives of all men who have been, like Xavier and Schwartz, greatly beloved by man as well as by God. Much of their work seems to vanish with them, reappearing after a time under humbler forms.

NOTE D. — Page 62.

" THE poetry of the Psalms is formed, not like
that of modern languages, by the response of
answering syllables, but of answering thoughts. This
peculiar form of composition was perhaps originally
founded upon that correspondence which a devout
soul perceives to exist in all the creation of God,
between the thing seen and unseen, — a correspondence upon which the teaching of all our Lord's
parables is grounded. The two things, the thing ex-
pressing and the thing expressed, *exist together, side
by side in fact,* and so they fall together, by a natural
process, *side by side,* in the poetry which describes
them. Thus in Psalm ciii. verses 11 – 13 :

The height of the heavens illustrates the boundless nature of
    God's mercy:
The expanse from east to west the distance to which he has
    removed our sins.
            The love and pity of an earthly father:
            The love and pity of a Heavenly one.

" ' *So consider the works of the Most High, and
there are two and two, one against another.*' (Ecclus.
xxxiii. 15.) " — *Plain Commentary on the Psalms.*

Note E. — Page 63.

OBSERVE what vivid brightness was cast upon all parts of the Old Testament at the first appearing of the Son of God, and learn from this what will be the radiance of the Scriptures at His Second Advent. The true disciples under the Old Covenant were ever waiting, "searching," as St. Peter says, "to discover what the Spirit which was in them did signify, when it testified beforehand the sufferings of Christ, and the glory which should follow." But looking back to the time of Jeremiah, the Maccabees, or that of the Second Temple, how strange must many passages of Scripture, now sparkling before our eyes with divine lustre, have appeared to the rationalist of the ancient synagogue! How puerile in some parts, how exaggerated and inexplicable in others, how devoid of learning and utility must have appeared to them many chapters and verses which at this day feed our faith, and fill us with a sense of the majestic unity of Scripture, cause our tears to flow, and bring weary and heavy-laden sinners to the feet of Jesus. What said they to Isaiah liii., to Psalms xxii., lxix., and many others? How strange and little worthy of the Lord must have appeared much that was contained in these, and in other psalms, prophecies, and types descriptive of Him. Yet what gospel truth has come forth from these! What unfolding of redeeming love! Let us there-

K

fore await even more glorious revelations in the day when our Master shall descend from heaven, for, says Irenæus, " the Scriptures contain difficulties which grace even now enables us to resolve ; but there are others which we leave to God, not only as respects this generation, but those to come, in order that it may be *God perpetually teaching, and man perpetually learning* from God the things that are of God."

Yet then shall we see the full meaning of many prophecies, facts, and instructions, whose Divine character is now only seen in detached features : then will be known the import of those parables, even now so impressive, of the fig-tree, — of the master returning from a far country, — of the bridegroom and bride, — of the net drawn to the shore of eternity, — of Lazarus, — of the guests, — of the husbandmen and of the marriage-feast. Then will be known all the glory of such expressions as these : " The Lord said unto my Lord, ' Sit thou at my right hand, until thine enemies be made thy footstool.'" " Thy people, Lord, shall be willing in the day of thy power." " The dew of thy youth shall be of the womb of the morning." " He shall wound the head of him who rules over a great country." " IIe shall drink of the brook in the way, therefore shall he lift up the head."

Then also thou wilt reveal thyself to us in all thy glory, Lord Jesus, Saviour, Comforter, Friend of the desolate, our Lord and our God ! Thou who hast seen death, but who art alive forevermore. Then

will all the knowledge of heaven be centred in Thyself, — the knowledge which the Holy Ghost even
now imparts, the knowledge in which Scripture even
now instructs us, for "*the testimony of Jesus is the
spirit of prophecy.*" — *See conclusion of Theopneustia.*

———◆———

Note F. — Page 86.

SEE on this text a sermon by Krummacher. —
Tower Church Sermons.

———◆———

Note G. — Page 101.

IT is often through the sore trouble of the soul that
the spirit, the part of us in which God lives,
is renewed from day to day. When "God," says
Jeremy Taylor, "would save man, he did it *by way
of a man*"; yet devotional authors seem little familiar with that fearful and beautiful thing, our sensitive
and rational nature, and in their writings slender
allowance is made for all that middle region of feelings and tendencies which, themselves neither good
nor evil, blend with and color for evil and for good
our whole spiritual life, with which they are linked
far more intimately than we imagine. In such writers, we trace but little communion with the joy and

sorrow and beauty of this earth, "glad, sad, and sweet," so that we sometimes wonder if they have known any enjoyments, pangs, or conflicts, but such as belong to the life that is in God. To be assured that they had joyed and sorrowed, and loved as men and women, and *as such* had felt Christ's unspeakable consolations, would be a touch of nature making them our kin. But it seldom comes. St. Thomas à Kempis, for instance, dismisses a whole world of feeling in two lines, "Love no woman in particular, but commend all good women in general to God." In Madame Guyon and Edwards we long, and long in vain, to see the hand of a man under the wings of the cherubim, and to feel its pressure. There is something deeply consoling in a betrayal of personal feeling, as when Doddridge laments for his little daughter. "This day my heart hath been almost torn in pieces by sorrow, yet sorrow so softened and so sweetened, that I number it among the best days of my life. Doest thou well to be angry for the gourd? God knows I am not angry, *but sorrowful he surely allows me to be.* Lord, give unto me a holy acquiescence of soul in thee, and now that my gourd is withered, shelter me under the shadow of thy wings." Here we see the man (most a saint in being most a man) agonized like his Master, and like him strengthened from on high, but by One greater than the angel.

Note H. — Page 111.

WHILE, as regards the great essentials of Christianity, things remain as they are,* not as we wish, conceive, or think of them, we cannot but perceive a diversity in the way in which we are led up to them, which answers to the infinite variety of the human spirit. We see how the great Apostle of the Gentiles, determined as he was to know and preach nothing among them but Christ and Him crucified, knew at the same time how to be all things to all men, meeting each one upon his peculiar ground, while he held his own with immovable tenacity. As that which he had to declare remained fixed and absolute, he did not change the truth to render it acceptable to his hearers, but, as he himself words it, *he changed his voice*, so as to bring truth before them under the aspect to which native bias or previous training rendered them most open.

We find in Mysticism a tendency to trample out rather than to train and modify the bent of nature, and this from an ardent desire for union with the Divine essence, which touches at every point upon Pantheistic absorption, and tends to substitute a blank uniformity for the energy and feature of Christian life. "Because I live," saith our Lord, "ye shall live also," and *as living*, be partakers in that which belongs to Life. — freedom, expansion, and variety.

* Taylor.

It has been often remarked, that each one among the branches of our Lord's great family preserves some portion of His teaching more faithfully, reflects some aspect of his character more clearly, than is done by the rest ; and passing from churches to individuals, we shall find that they who are in Christ will resemble *each other in so much as* they resemble him ; they will be like each other (as in earthly relationships) without being alike.   Our natural characteristics are not obliterated ; rather is the man renewed after Christ's likeness restored to *Himself*, that excellent thing for which God made him at the first, the type from which he had consciously fallen away.

—◆—

Note I.—Page 137.

WHEN, and to whom, has the perfect circle of Truth been visible?   Certain portions of it seem always in the shade, though no portion of it can remain there long.   It seems God's will that earnest and faithful-minded men should be continually from age to age bringing forward such fragments of it as have fastened on their own minds in such strong and (relatively) undue prominence, that they are constrained to present them to the world as they arise, where, like plants set in the ground with reference to fitness of clime and season, *they* wither, but not before they have fructified and shed seed, which, falling on a more prepared soil, brings forth fruit to perfection.

The heat and extravagance with which it was at first accompanied fall off like husks from the ripened ear, and the truth which these have kept warm, while it had to push its way through cold, earthy obstructions, unfolds in its fulness. In the physical world this holds true of the secrets which disentangled themselves from the follies of alchemy, and perhaps applies to many systems of our present day, which, containing a vital essence of truth, overlaid with much that is fantastic, will themselves die out; yet, under other conditions, exert an influence on general science. So in the moral and spiritual world we see forms perishing *because* of the life that is in them. We say Quakerism has decayed and dwindled; but why? even because the wide and loving principles it promulgated in an age of dreary spiritual exclusivism, have been, since the days of the Early Friends (the first apostles of so many a holy cause), gradually and silently incorporated into the thoughts of Christian men in general. *They*, as Howitt says, have missed being a great people, but the truths they so simply and perseveringly advocated have *not* failed of their mark. Neander, speaking of reformers of the heart only, guided by the pure will without the reflective wisdom, says, "Their efforts are as a fire catching rapidly at all around it, but working rather destructively than as an abiding warmth or a clear, diffusive blaze. . . . Before the coming of a great light, its approach is heralded by lesser lights, which, after shining in the darkness, seem to disappear. Before a decisive and general triumph of the right, its way is first cleansed by the blood of victims who have fallen in its cause, and by attempts that miscarry because they were untimely. But a voice from the Past (the world's history) assures us that he who goeth forth to do battle for the right simply is sure of victory, as, although he should be himself over-powered, and his work for a season defeated, he has yet thereby contributed to the final triumph of the right in its proper time."

The design of the Almighty is like that of the vast cathedrals of old at which many generations of work-men were content to labor in succession; each help-ing to carry out some part of the magnificent plan, each building up some part of his life and strength in the mighty structure whose completion he could never hope to witness.

> " They shall perish, but thou remainest;
> And they all shall wax old as a garment,
> And as a vesture shalt thou fold them up,
> And they are changed;
> But thou art the same; and thy years shall not fail;
> *The children of thy servants shall continue,*
> *And their seed shall stand fast in thy sight.*"

—◆—

Note K. — Page 144.

" AND I, my loving Brentius," writes Luther, " to the end that I may the better under-stand this case, do use to think in this manner, namely, as if in my heart were no quality or virtue at all which is called faith or love, but I set all on Christ, and say, my *formalis justitia*, that is my sure, my constant and complete righteousness, in which there is no want or failing, but is, as before God it ought to be, Christ my Lord and Saviour."

Faith saves us ; but how ? — by making us aware of Christ, who saves. Faith does not *make* things what they are, but *shows* us them as they are in Christ. Certain systems lay a pressure upon the subjective side greater than the spirit of man is at all times able to bear; working out all things from the depths of individual consciousness, *as if truths were not there at all until they are (manifestly) there for us.* Wesley, for instance, felt and preached Christ both freely and fully ; yet, from the central importance his teaching gives to a conscious spiritual work in man, it tends, in some degree, to withdraw the soul's eye from Christ, to fix it upon what is going on within itself.

Happy for us, if Christ can look there and find his own image reflected, however faintly ; but *we* must look at Him, at the sun in the heavens, not at the sun in the brook, its broken and ever-varying reflection. So long as we are resting in anything within ourselves, be it even in a work of grace, there remains, at least to honest hearts, a ground for continual restlessness and continual disappointment. To know that we have nothing, are nothing out of Christ, is to know the truth which makes us free.

8

Note L. — Page 147.

THE Christian's life is no Drama planned to correspond with certain prescribed Unities of time and situation; but, *because it is a life*, it is too solemn, too real a thing to be bounded by any such limitations. The Bible prescribes no fixed routine of religious experience, and I know not how to express my sense of the crudity, I would also say cruelty, of such religious writings as insist upon certain phases of feeling as being essential to every true conversion; thus making sad the heart of the righteous whom God hath not made sad. " *The Gods,*" said the wise Heathen, " *give not all things to men at all times.*" Have Christians yet to learn that certain feelings are only proper, say rather are only *possible* to certain stages of experience? *That when we are able to receive things we do receive them,* and until then must be content to wait, *abiding in the truth,* growing up in it from day to day, but forcing nothing either upon ourselves or others.

How carefully should we guard against the passing of a religious truth into a religious conventionalism! The deepest expressions of feeling, as when St. Paul, seeing so far into his own nature, and into God's purity, *is able* to call himself the chief of sinners, become *false, commonplace,* when taken up by those who do not feel, but merely repeat them — when they are out of all harmony with the life and consciousness of the speaker.

We may apply this also to the crude admonitions
so often addressed to afflicted people; the set phrases
in which, without any consideration of his fitness to
receive such sayings, the sufferer is referred to the
will of God, the love of Christ, for compensation.
Yet the loss of a felt, experienced good, even
of an earthly kind, can only be made
up for by a comfort equally felt
and experienced, *and how
can that be a comfort
which has never
been a joy?*

Cambridge : Stereotyped and Printed by Welch, Bigelow, & Co.

Lightning Source UK Ltd.
Milton Keynes UK
10 November 2009

146012UK00001B/50/A